RAND NATIONAL SECURITY RESEARCH DIVISION



# Fiscal Performance and U.S. International Influence

C. Richard Neu, Zhimin Mao, Ian P. Cook

This research was conducted within the RAND National Security Research Division (NSRD) of the RAND Corporation. NSRD conducts research and analysis on defense and national security topics for the U.S. and allied defense, foreign policy, homeland security, and intelligence communities and foundations and other nongovernmental organizations that support defense and national security analysis.

**Library of Congress Cataloging-in-Publication Data**

**ISBN: 978-0-8330-8171-1**

The RAND Corporation is a nonprofit institution that helps improve policy and decisionmaking through research and analysis. RAND's publications do not necessarily reflect the opinions of its research clients and sponsors.

Support RAND—make a tax-deductible charitable contribution at
www.rand.org/giving/contribute.html



RAND OFFICES

SANTA MONICA, CA • WASHINGTON, DC

PITTSBURGH, PA • NEW ORLEANS, LA • JACKSON, MS • BOSTON, MA

DOHA, QA • CAMBRIDGE, UK • BRUSSELS, BE

www.rand.org

# Preface

U.S. fiscal performance—the evolution of federal budget deficits and debt and the political process for dealing with both—is a topic of considerable public interest today. Much has been written about the origins of the current high level of U.S. federal debt, its possible consequences, and proposed approaches to reducing it. This report focuses on a particular aspect of the U.S. fiscal situation that has received less attention: the consequences of the federal debt for U.S. international influence. The report explores the possible effects of government debt on U.S. military and economic power. It should be of interest to both policymakers and the parts of the general public interested in the consequences of high levels of government debt.

This report is a product of the RAND Corporation's continuing program of self-initiated independent research. Support for such research is provided, in part, by donors and by the independent research and development provisions of RAND's contracts for the operation of its U.S. Department of Defense federally funded research and development centers. The research was conducted within the RAND National Security Research Division (NSRD) of the RAND Corporation. NSRD conducts research and analysis on defense and national security topics for the U.S. and allied defense, foreign policy, homeland security, and intelligence communities and foundations and other nongovernmental organizations that support defense and national security analysis.

For more information on the RAND National Security Research Division, see www.rand.org/nsrd/ or contact the Director (contact information is provided on web page).

# Contents

# Figures

# Tables

# Summary

ADM Mike Mullen has argued, while he was Chairman of the Joint Chiefs of Staff and many times since he left that post, that, "Our national debt is our biggest national security threat."[1] At one level, Admiral Mullen's statement is obvious: The difficult U.S. fiscal position and efforts to rectify it constrain government spending for many purposes, including spending for national security. Defense spending has already been cut significantly—from previously projected levels—under the provisions of the Budget Control Act of 2011.

Judgments differ on the consequences of these defense spending reductions for U.S. military capabilities and for national security more generally. Budget constraints have been sufficient, however, to motivate a major adjustment in U.S. national security guidance.[2] In a letter attached to that guidance, then–Secretary of Defense Leon Panetta said, in particular, that the new strategy recognizes that "the Joint Force of the future will be smaller and leaner."

Beyond their direct affect on military spending, high government debt and the steps necessary to reduce this debt to sustainable levels may be undermining the economic instruments of U.S. power and the U.S. ability to shape global conditions through other than military means.

This report explores the possible linkages between high government debt and plausible instruments of U.S. international influence. Our principal finding is that, to date, high debt levels have not had clearly negative consequences for U.S. international influence. There are, however, some worrying indications that this may change in the future.

## Some Basic Facts About U.S. Government Debt

Figure S.1 shows the evolution of U.S. federal debt held by the public and gross general government debt. The former concept is the common "headline" definition of federal debt. The latter concept includes debt of state and local governments and federal debt held by government trust funds; this is the definition of government debt commonly used for international comparisons. While general government debt is higher, the two definitions of debt show the same historical pattern and are, for most analytic purposes, interchangeable.

After reaching a low point, as a percentage of gross domestic product (GDP), in fiscal year (FY) 2001, U.S. federal debt has risen rapidly to a level not seen since shortly after World War II. Among the factors that contributed to the higher debt were tax reductions enacted in 2001

1 Laura Basset, "Adm. Mike Mullen: 'National Debt Is Our Biggest Security Threat,'" *Huffington Post*, June 24, 2010.

2 U.S. Department of Defense, *Sustaining U.S. Global Leadership: Priorities for 21st Century Defense*, Washington, D.C., January 2012.

**Figure S.1**
**Federal Debt Held by the Public and Gross General Government Debt**

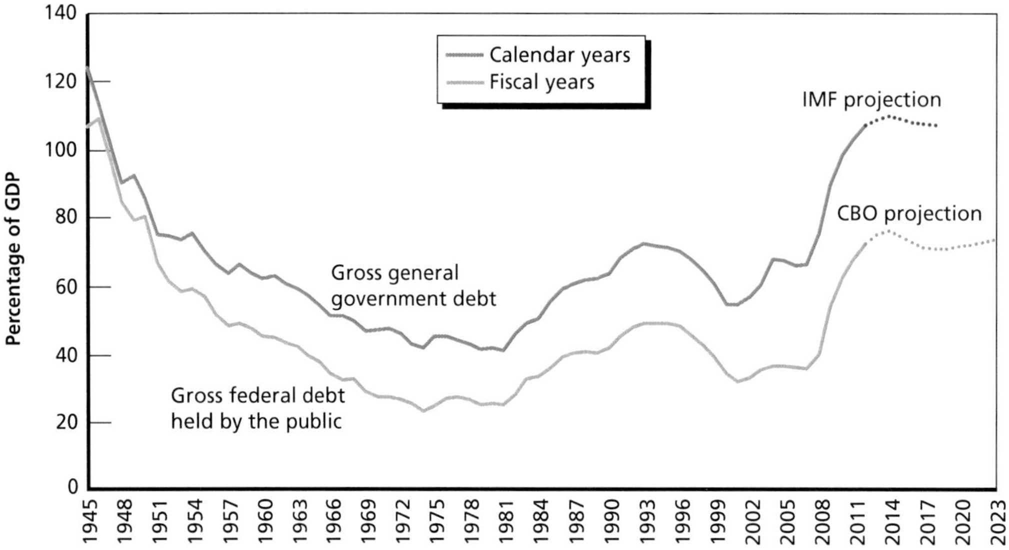


SOURCES: Congressional Budget Office, *Updated Budget Projections: Fiscal Years 2013 to 2023*, Washington, D.C., May 14, 2013; Federal Reserve System Board of Governors, "Flow of Funds Accounts of the United States: Historical Data," in *Release Z.1, Financial Accounts of the United States*, various dates; and International Monetary Fund, *Fiscal Monitor: Fiscal Adjustment in an Uncertain World*, Washington, D.C., April 2013.
RAND *RR353-S.1*

and 2003 (the so-called Bush-era tax cuts), rapidly rising costs for social entitlement programs, increased outlays for military operations in Iraq and Afghanistan, reduced revenues because of the major recession that began in 2008, and aggressive fiscal stimulus measures put in place in 2009 to combat the recession. Outlays for operations in Iraq and Afghanistan are now coming down, stimulus spending has largely run its course, major reductions in discretionary federal spending have been enacted, and some of the Bush-era tax cuts have expired, but the debt will continue to rise through FY 2014. More troubling, the Congressional Budget Office projects that, *even with the full spending reductions required by the sequester*, federal debt will dip only temporarily before the fiscal consequences of an aging population force it higher again.[3]

## Consequences of Government Debt for the Economic Instruments of U.S. Power

The principal basis for U.S. economic power is the simple size of the U.S. economy. The economics profession is beginning to understand that high levels of debt can slow economic growth, especially when gross general government debt surpasses 85 or 90 percent of GDP.[4] U.S. government debt crossed this threshold in 2009, and the negative consequences, if any, for U.S. economic growth probably still lie out in the future.

[3] Congressional Budget Office, *Updated Budget Projections: Fiscal Years 2013 to 2023*, Washington, D.C., May 14, 2013.

[4] See, for example, Stephen G. Cecchetti, M. S. Mohanty, and Fabrizio Zampolli, *The Real Effects of Debt*, Basel, Switzerland: Bank for International Settlements, Working Paper 352, September 2011.

If government debt does eventually slow U.S. economic growth, it will reinforce a trend that has been under way for some years. After holding steady for two decades, the U.S. share of global output has been declining since 1999, or since 2005, discounting the effects of the technology boom in the late 1990s (Figure S.2). The shares of traditional U.S. allies—the European Union and Japan—have been falling even longer, while the shares of China, India, and Russia have been rising.

Also damaging to economic growth is uncertainty over future government economic policy, heightened as a result of confrontations between the White House and Congress over budget matters. Economists at Stanford University and the University of Chicago estimate that the increase in policy uncertainty from 2006 to August 2011 (at the time of the political showdown over the federal debt ceiling) can be expected to foreshadow a decline of more than 2 percent in GDP.[5]

As the U.S. share of global output has fallen, so has the U.S. share of world trade, reducing the ability of the United States to shape the rules of the international trading system. Voting shares in major international financial institutions, such as the International Monetary Fund and the World Bank, are tied to shares of global output and trade; consequently, the United States has seen some erosion of its formal influence in these bodies.

Since U.S. government debt began to rise after 2001, the value of the dollar has declined by 26 percent in price-adjusted terms against the currencies of major U.S. trading partners. The U.S. Federal Reserve Board's very aggressive action to push down dollar interest rates,

**Figure S.2**
**Shares of Global GDP, Selected Countries (at purchasing power parity exchange rates)**

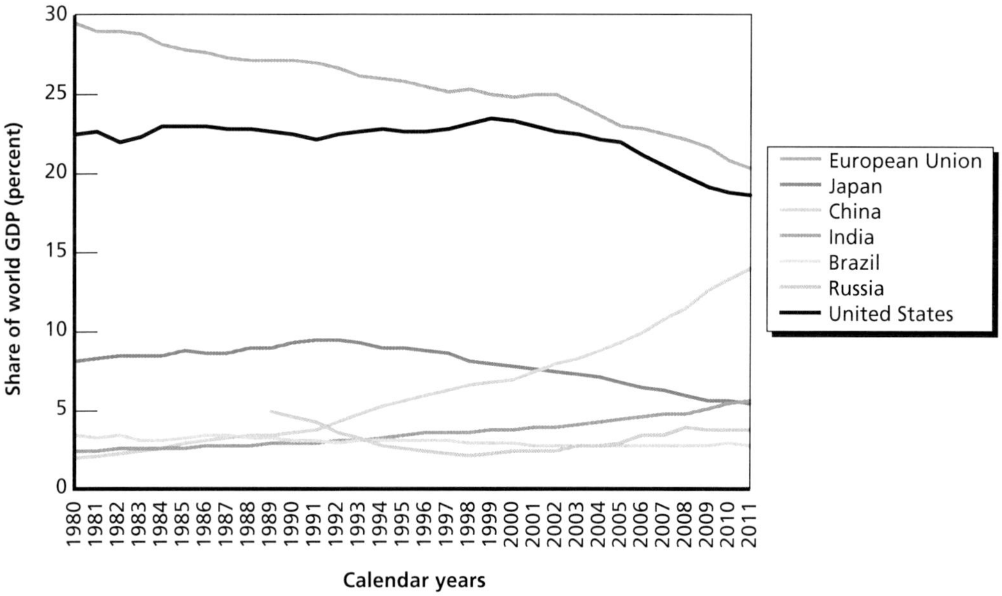


SOURCE: International Bank for Reconstruction and Development, "World Development Indicators," database, April 16, 2013.
RAND *RR353-S.2*

[5] Scott R. Baker, Nicholas Bloom, and Steven J. Daly, *Measuring Economic Policy Uncertainty*, Economic Policy Uncertainty website, working paper, April 29, 2013.

rather than persistent fiscal imbalances, is the most likely explanation of the dollar's weakness, however, and there is no clear link between the value of the dollar and U.S. ability to shape world events. Neither the dollar's position as the world's dominant reserve currency nor the share of foreign exchange transactions involving the dollar—both more plausibly related to U.S. economic interests and influence in the world—has changed significantly since U.S. government debt began to grow rapidly after 2001. U.S. financial institutions retain the confidence of international investors. The share of cross-border bank deposits held in U.S. banks has risen during the period of growing U.S. government debt.

## Debt and Investment in the Nation's Future

The relationship between government debt levels and investments that are important for the nation's future is ambiguous. Throughout the period since the end of World War II, private domestic investment has shown a distinct negative correlation with government debt levels (Figure S.3). From 2010 through 2012, however, this pattern has been broken, with private investment rising, although government debt also continued.

Federal outlays for human capital development (education and training, employment, and social services) rose sharply in FYs 2009 and 2010 as part of the fiscal stimulus program that aimed to counter the ill effects of the Great Recession. But outlays for these purposes fell just as sharply in FYs 2011 and 2012, when the stimulus program had run its course. The

**Figure S.3**
**U.S. Private Investment and Gross General Government Debt (calendar years)**

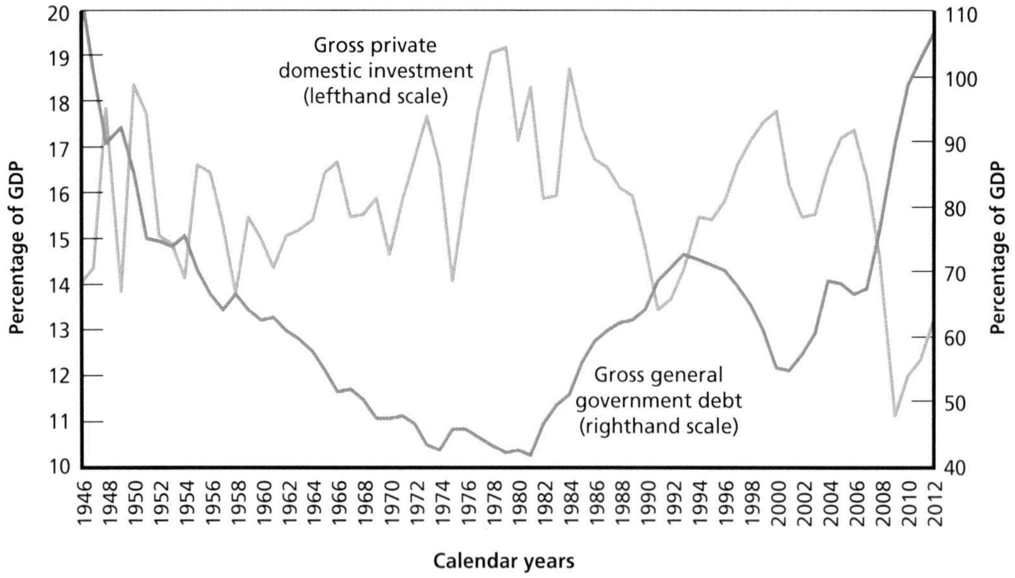


SOURCE: U.S. Department of Commerce, Bureau of Economic Analysis, *National Income and Product Accounts Tables*, webpage, May 2013, Table 5.1, and Federal Reserve System Board of Governors, *Release Z.1*, various dates.
RAND *RR353-S.3*

Office of Management and Budget (OMB) projects that these outlays will decline further in real terms through FY 2018.[6]

Federal spending for major capital projects (including grants to states for such projects) showed some upward movement as a share of GDP as the federal debt grew from FY 2001 through FY 2010. But since then, it has stalled.[7] Federal spending for this purpose is dominated by military-related capital projects, and the stagnation in this account is mostly a result of slower growth of military capital projects. Federal investments in nonmilitary capital projects have remained generally stable as a share of GDP since the early 1990s. No projections of federal capital spending in future years are available.

Federal outlays for research and development seem to have been unaffected by rising federal debt, remaining roughly constant as a fraction of GDP since the early 1990s.[8]

## What Might Have Happened

Economic power (or any sort of national power, for that matter) is exercised best in the process of creating institutions and conditions that advance U.S. national interests and simultaneously benefit the global community. Historically, the United States has used its economic strength and influence to play leading and constructive roles in creating, shaping, or sustaining numerous important international institutions, programs, and initiatives.

But what has the United States accomplished recently? Have high government debt and a political system seemingly incapable of resolving disputes over fiscal policy undermined the U.S. ability or willingness to exercise international leadership? The record since 2001 is mixed.

The United States has organized effective international economic sanctions against Iran, for example. Some U.S. proposals on international financial regulation—requiring large financial institutions to plan in advance for resolving their own affairs in the event of future crises, for example—have gained international support. Other proposals—separation of commercial and investment banking and limitations on proprietary trading—have fared less well however. Innovative U.S. legal approaches to enforcing international financial sanctions and combatting money laundering are being copied abroad.

But the United States has been conspicuously absent from international schemes to increase the resources available to the International Monetary Fund, while potential rivals for international influence—China, Russia, and Saudi Arabia—have pledged support. The United States has not provided financial support to indebted allies during the Eurozone debt crisis. On at least one occasion, policy advice from senior U.S. officials to Eurozone governments was rejected with sharp references to the U.S. inability to control its own borrowing. More recently, however, U.S. urging that Europe should temper austerity measures has gained some support. The United States has not been able to convince other nations to bring the Doha Round of multilateral trade negotiations to a successful conclusion, but the United States has taken a leading role in creating a trans-Pacific trading arrangement and a U.S.–European Union trade pact. U.S. economic difficulties have precluded broad financial assistance to countries trying

---

6 OMB, *The President's Budget for Fiscal Year 2014, Historical Tables*, April 2013b, Table 8.7.

7 OMB, 2013b, Table 9.3.

8 OMB, 2013b, Table 9.7.

to transform their economies after the Arab Spring. Fiscal constraints have also diminished U.S. capacity to resolve important domestic issues—high costs for poor health care outcomes, weak public education systems, growing income inequality, for example—risking the social and political cohesion at home necessary to deal confidently and effectively with the rest of the world.

Some prominent commentators (see specific references in Chapter Six of this report) have argued that the United States is withdrawing from world leadership, that fiscal problems have forced it to limit military responses to international security challenges, and that the U.S. voice in international affairs has been diminished. We do not find clear evidence to support these propositions, but neither can we reject them convincingly. Certainly, the U.S. fiscal predicament cannot be strengthening U.S. international influence.

## What Is to Be Done?

The Unites States faces a dilemma. A persistently high level of government debt threatens future economic growth and constrains the ability of the government to act in pursuit of national interests, both international and domestic. Yet efforts to bring down the debt will further constrain government outlays and action—possibly for many years into the future. History suggests that countries seldom grow their way out of burdensome debt. Actions to increase government revenues or constrain expenditures are necessary. Undoubtedly, there is room to increase government revenues, particularly by eliminating unproductive tax preferences. But spending restraint will also have to play a major role.

Opportunities to reduce discretionary expenditures further are limited. Discretionary expenditures, defense and nondefense, today account for less than 7 percent of GDP, less than one-half the share of entitlement spending. Constraining entitlement spending will minimize the need to reduce outlays that contribute directly to U.S. international influence—defense, international representation, and assistance—and that create future productive capacity—investments in infrastructure, research and development, and education. Unfortunately, current legislation is exactly the reverse of this. The Budget Control Act mandates restraint in discretionary spending only; spending for entitlements is exempt from cuts. Preserving U.S. international influence will require a different approach.

# Acknowledgments

The authors are grateful for insightful and rigorous reviews of a draft of this paper by Roger Kubarych and Howard Shatz. Their comments were constructive and challenging, and our attempts to respond to these comments—successful, we hope—strengthened the paper considerably. At an earlier stage, we also received valuable guidance from our colleague James Dobbins, at that time the director of the International Security and Defense Policy Center within RAND's National Security Research Division.

We also benefited from the opportunity to present early findings to our RAND colleagues in a work-in-progress seminar. Few organizations can assemble a group of experts with such breadth and depth of knowledge. This paper is undoubtedly the better for having been produced within the RAND environment.

Any errors of fact or judgment that remain despite the best efforts of our colleagues and reviewers are the responsibility of the authors.

## Abbreviations

| | |
|---|---|
| BIS | Bank for International Settlements |
| CBO | Congressional Budget Office |
| DoD | U.S. Department of Defense |
| EU | European Union |
| FY | fiscal year |
| FYDP | Future Years Defense Program |
| GDP | gross domestic product |
| IMF | International Monetary Fund |
| NAB | New Arrangements to Borrow |
| OCO | overseas contingency operation |
| OECD | Organization for Economic Cooperation and Development |
| OMB | Office of Management and Budget |
| QE2, QE3, QE4 | successive rounds of quantitative easing by the U.S. Federal Reserve |
| R&D | research and development |
| RDT&E | research, development, test, and evaluation |
| UK | United Kingdom |
| VAR | vector autoregression |
| WTO | World Trade Organization |

CHAPTER ONE

# Introduction

Our national debt is our biggest national security threat.
*ADM Mike Mullen,*
*then-Chairman of the Joint Chiefs of Staff,*
*June 2010*[1]

Admiral Mullen's warning is frequently quoted, but seldom carefully examined. Just how does U.S. government debt threaten U.S. national security or U.S. international interests more broadly?

At one level, Admiral Mullen's statement is obvious: High debt levels and concerns about yet higher levels in the future constrain U. S. government spending for many purposes, including spending for national security. And the measures necessary to reduce government debt will require substantial reductions in spending, at least for some time. These reductions are already happening. The Budget Control Act of 2011 (P.L. 112-25), a direct response to congressional demands for fiscal restraint, has resulted in significant reductions in previously planned defense spending and other "discretionary" federal outlays stretching over ten years.[2]

The extent to which these spending reductions will cut into U.S. defense capabilities is contentious. Military power does not vanish overnight, and the military superiority that the United States enjoys today can withstand temporary reductions in resources. If spending reductions persist, however, and if they are pursued far enough, U.S. capacity for military action will eventually decline, as force structures shrink and modernization is delayed. The nonselective and misallocated character of mandated spending reductions compounds their negative consequences. These reductions in military spending are already having consequences for the deployment of U.S. forces, their operating tempos, and their training activities.[3]

---

[1] Laura Basset, "Adm. Mike Mullen: 'National Debt Is Our Biggest Security Threat,'" *Huffington Post*, June 24, 2010. Admiral Mullen has made similar comments many times; this is among the earliest press reports.

[2] As the term is used in a federal budgetary context, *discretionary spending* refers to federal outlays that are set on an annual basis. The complement to discretionary spending is *mandatory spending*, which is automatically obligated as a result of previously enacted laws. Mandatory spending includes interest on the federal debt and so-called entitlement programs, such as Medicare, Medicaid, Social Security, and veterans' benefits. Discretionary spending is "everything else." In fiscal year (FY) 2011—the last before the spending reductions the Budget Control Act mandated—discretionary outlays accounted for 37 percent of all federal outlays.

[3] Senior defense officials characterize budget cuts in FY 2013 as forcing the U.S. military to "burn readiness." See U.S. Department of Defense (DoD), *News Briefing by Under Secretary of Defense Hale and Lt. General Ramsay on the Fiscal Year Defense Budget Proposal*, April 10, 2013b.

Beyond the consequences of spending reductions necessary to control or reduce government debt, the simple existence of high levels of government debt and a political process seemingly unable to control deficits and debt will also have more subtle effects. At some point, for example, rising debt levels will limit U.S. capabilities to respond to future challenges—security challenges, natural disasters, financial crises, etc.—with vigorous government action. Britain's former prime minister Gordon Brown called efforts to control government debt "prudence with a purpose," the purpose being to have sufficient ammunition to fight crises or wars.[4]

Further, evidence is emerging that high levels of government debt are associated with slower economic growth in subsequent years—especially when debt exceeds certain thresholds.[5] Although the mechanisms by which debt affects growth have not been fully worked out, some plausible explanations can be put forward. The need to finance government deficits, for example, crowds out productive private-sector investment in some circumstances. Uncertainty about the spending or tax policies that will eventually be necessary to control or reduce debt can discourage business investment and induce households to save rather than spend. Constraints on government spending because of the real or perceived dangers of high debt levels limit government investments in infrastructure and education, with deleterious consequences for future growth. And high levels of government debt limit the tools available to national authorities for dealing with an economic downturn. (The current level of U.S. federal debt, for example, has rendered further fiscal stimulus politically impossible.)

To the extent that the current high level of U.S. government debt impinges on economic growth, the result will be a U.S. economy that is smaller than it might otherwise have been. And a smaller economy is, almost by definition, one that matters less in the world, particularly if other economies continue to grow. A smaller national economy supports less action—military or otherwise—on the global stage and affords the U.S. government less influence in international economic, commercial, and political affairs. Similarly, if high debt levels or efforts to reduce them constrain outlays for foreign assistance, diplomacy, and other forms of international representation, U.S. international engagement and influence will decrease.

Other consequences of high debt levels or spending reductions associated with debt reduction efforts are necessarily more speculative. High debt and a political process incapable of reducing it, for example, may sap foreign confidence in the United States, rendering the U.S.

---

4 The quotation from Brown and the interpretation of what he meant are from Chris Giles, "Austerity Is Hurting, But Is It Working?" *Financial Times*, April 27, 2013.

5 See, for example, Stephen G. Cecchetti, M. S. Mohanty, and Fabrizio Zampolli, *The Real Effects of Debt*, Bank for International Settlements (BIS), Working Paper 352, September 2011; Carmen M. Reinhart and Kenneth S. Rogoff, "Growth in a Time of Debt," *American Economic Review: Papers and Proceedings*, Vol. 100, No. 2, May 2010, pp. 573–578; Carmen M. Reinhart and Kenneth S. Rogoff, *This Time Is Different: Eight Centuries of Financial Folly*, Princeton University Press, 2009; Carmen M. Reinhart, Vincent R. Reinhart, and Kenneth S. Rogoff, "Public Debt Overhangs: Advanced Economy Episodes Since 1800," *Journal of Economic Perspectives*, Summer 2012, pp. 69–86; and Mohan Kumar and Jaejoon Woo, *Public Debt and Growth*, International Monetary Fund (IMF) Working Paper WP/10/174, July 1, 2010.

Some aspects of the analysis in Reinhart and Rogoff, 2010, have been questioned. See Thomas Herndon, Michael Ash, and Robert Pollin, *Does High Public Debt Consistently Stifle Economic Growth? A Critique of Reinhart and Rogoff*, Working Paper Number 322, Political Economy Research Institute, University of Massachusetts Amherst, April 2013. Opinion remains divided on whether errors discovered or alleged in this paper seriously undermine its conclusions. In any event, the other references cited here apparently remain valid and support the propositions that high levels of government debt can depress subsequent economic growth and that the negative effects of debt increase when this debt passes certain thresholds.

government, U.S. political leaders, and U.S. economic actors less influential in world affairs.[6] Further, inability to resolve fiscal difficulties and the perceived shortage of public resources that comes from high debt may undermine American self-confidence, leaving the country less willing to accept costs or risks to advance its interests abroad or to pursue initiatives for the benefit of the global community. High debt and subsequent slower growth may also reduce the U.S. role in key international economic activities—international trade, banking, and finance, for example—either directly because the United States plays a less prominent role in these activities or indirectly because domestic or international confidence in U.S. capabilities or policies is impaired. And if high debt postpones resolution of domestic social or economic problems, the internal cohesion necessary for effective external action may eventually be undermined. In short, failure to put U.S. fiscal affairs on a sustainable path may weaken the instruments of international influence that have served the United States well since the end of World War II.

Few would suggest that the United States faces significant risk of a major sovereign debt crisis—in the style of Greece, for example. Nonetheless, continuously rising debt may pose dangers that are less dramatic but just as real. In a recent article about the dangers to Japan of its own government debt—higher as a percentage of gross domestic product (GDP) than the U.S. debt—Adam Posen, the president of the Peterson Institute for International Economics, sums up the consequences of persistently high government debt for large, developed countries: "When a large country with its own currency reaches its fiscal limit, growth ends not with a bang but a whimper of declining vitality and diminishing resilience."[7]

This report is an attempt to assess the extent to which government budgetary problems in the United States—primarily at the level of the federal government—may be affecting the nation's ability to maintain and to project both military and economic power. There are, of course, no simple operational metrics for military power, economic power, or international influence, and we cannot plot declining or rising U.S. influence in particular historical periods. What we can do, however, is try to assess the extent to which U.S. fiscal difficulties are weakening key *instruments* of international influence. In some cases, we can also cite particular instances in which U.S. international leadership seems less pronounced than it might have been in the absence of large government debts. Even if the consequences of government debt remain speculative, prudence requires being alert to the risks these debts pose and looking for evidence that these risks may become troublesome in the future.

Our focus on government debt is not meant to minimize the potential dangers of excessive corporate, household, or financial-system debt. Indeed, the global financial crisis that contributed importantly to today's high level of government debt had its origins in unsustainable mortgage debts and the highly leveraged condition of many financial institutions. Evidence is mounting that excessive levels of any kind of debt—government, corporate, household, financial institution—can be harmful. The general proposition is that high levels of noncontingent liabilities (debt) can have the same consequences at the level of the national economy that

---

[6] The inability of the U.S. political process to deal with high deficits and debt may be as damaging as the debt itself. In a recent paper, Robert Zoellick, former president of the World Bank, quotes Australian Foreign Minister Bob Carr: "The United States is one budget deal away from restoring its global preeminence." See Robert Zoellick, "The Currency of Power," *Foreign Policy*, November 2012, pp. 67–73. The Associated Press quoted Carr somewhat more pungently on a different occasion: "America is just one budget deal away from ending all talk of America being in decline." See "Bob Carr Denies Romney Diplomatic Gaffe," *Australian Times*, July 23, 2012.

[7] Adam Posen, "Japan Should Rethink Its Stimulus," *Financial Times*, January 16, 2013.

leverage has for an investment portfolio: The effects of positive and negative developments are magnified.[8] This increases the potential for macroeconomic instability, which in turn inhibits investment and future growth. Although the consequences of household and corporate debt are important subjects for study, this report takes a narrower perspective, focusing on government debt. This is because government debt impinges particularly on functions reserved to the government, such as national security and international relations, which are the ultimate subjects of this exploration.

Our analysis here is largely exploratory, seeking indicators that plausibly reflect the effects of government deficits and debt on particular instruments of influence and on the U.S. ability and willingness to use these instruments. Happily, history does not provide enough examples of unsustainable fiscal policies—especially in the United States—to support firm conclusions about causality. Typically, we can observe only that certain developments have been contemporaneous with episodes of high government debt. Arguments about causality necessarily remain theoretical, ad hoc, and/or speculative.

Attributing causality is especially difficult at this moment in history. Virtually every country in the world suffered from the international financial crisis that began in 2007 and from the deep global recession that followed. Undoubtedly, crisis, recession, and the efforts of national authorities to mitigate their effects contributed importantly to the rise of government deficits and debts in the last few years. Are troubling developments, then, the consequences of deficits and debt, or are they the consequences of financial crisis and recession that contributed to these deficits and debts? Or are they due to yet other factors largely unrelated to any of these things? Ultimately, we cannot know. National economies do not present opportunities for controlled experiments. We are left with observing correlation or simultaneity of events and offering arguments about why they may or may not be causally related.

Neither can we attribute losses of international stature or influence that the United States may have suffered in recent years entirely to unsustainable fiscal policies. The prudential and regulatory failures that precipitated the recent financial crisis, for example, raise questions about the wisdom and effectiveness of U.S. financial policies. Similarly, failures to find weapons of mass destruction in Iraq and the drawn-out and so far indecisive conflicts in Iraq and Afghanistan have likely undermined U.S. leadership in international security affairs. The first decade of the current century has been a complicated period, and identifying direct causal links is impossible. But failing to look for such links would be at best imprudent.

Our principal finding is that there is little clear evidence to date that U.S. debt and deficits have substantially undermined the instruments of U.S. international influence. Perhaps this is not surprising, since high or unsustainable levels of debt are recent phenomena in the United States, and the painful measures necessary to reduce this debt are just beginning. There are, however, some indicators—particularly with regard to economic power—that suggest that negative consequences could grow in the future, if current budget problems are not resolved. In at least one sense, this report is well timed: Major damage has not yet been done, and there is still time to correct course.

The second chapter of this report presents a brief overview of the recent history of government finance in the United States, the resulting deficits and debt, and how recent deficits have been financed. Chapter Three discusses, at a high level of aggregation, the consequences to date

---

[8] Cecchetti, Mohanty, and Zampolli, 2011, makes this analogy to financial leverage.

**A Note on Budget Projections in This Report**

As this report was being written—May 2013—the outlook for U.S. federal spending was highly uncertain. In August 2011, Congress passed and the president signed the Budget Control Act of 2011 (P.L. 112-25).[a] This legislation mandated reductions of $917 billion in discretionary federal outlays—from previously projected levels—beginning in FY 2012 and extending through FY 2021. The legislation also mandated a further reduction of $1.2 trillion in discretionary outlays through FY 2021, to take effect January 1, 2013, if Congress and the White House had not agreed on some alternative deficit-reduction measures by that date. The Budget Control Act specified a particular division of the initial spending reductions between "security" and "nonsecurity" accounts in FYs 2012 and 2013. The second round of reductions—the so-called sequester—is to be divided equally between security and nonsecurity discretionary spending. Importantly, spending reductions in the second round are to be applied equally to all budget programs, projects, and activities (in popular usage, to each budget line item) in the respective security and nonsecurity accounts. No reprogramming of funding from one budget line item to another is permitted, foreclosing the possibility of protecting priority programs.

Subsequent legislation postponed the date for the sequester to March 1, 2013, and increased government revenues by allowing a temporary reduction in payroll taxes to expire and eliminating the so-called Bush-era income tax cuts for higher-income households. No alternative spending plan was enacted by March 1, and consequently the sequester went into effect. At this writing, Congress was debating whether to amend the sequester provisions, and it is possible that the full sequester or its across-the-board character will be only temporary.[b]

Detailed budgeting in this environment is obviously difficult. The President submitted his budget proposals for FY 2014 on April 10, somewhat later than current law calls for. With respect to overall federal deficits, the President's budget is roughly in line with the provisions of the Budget Control Act in that the budget foresees total deficit reductions over ten years of a bit more than the amount specified in that act. The President's budget, however, proposes to accomplish this deficit reduction differently than the way the Budget Control Act calls for. Specifically, the President's budget proposes higher revenues to relieve some of the spending constraints required under the terms of the sequester. The President's budget also proposes to replace the across-the-board spending reductions the act mandates with better targeted reductions that allow preservation of high-priority (in the administration's eyes) programs. Congressional Republicans continue to oppose increasing revenues, and which parts, if any, of the President's proposal Congress will accept remains to be seen. Without some budget deal, the sequester will remain in effect. Consequently, spending projections in the President's budget likely constitute upper limits.

The President's budget remains, however, the only available detailed plan for federal spending in future years. Unless otherwise noted, projections of future spending in this report reflect the President's FY 2014 budget proposal.

---

[a] For a summary of the Budget Control Act of 2011, see Bill Heniff, Jr., Elizabeth Rybicki, and Shannon M. Mahan, *The Budget Control Act of 2011*, Washington, D.C.: Congressional Research Service, R41965, August 2011.

[b] As of this writing, only a single exception to the across-the-board character of the sequester has been enacted. The Federal Aviation Administration has been permitted to reprogram funds to avoid furloughs of air traffic controllers.

of budget pressures on U.S. military spending, how this spending may evolve over the next few years, and how U.S. military strategy is being adjusted to accommodate reduced funding. Chapter Four cites emerging evidence about the possible effect of debt on overall economic growth and, more generally, discusses how current deficits and debt may be affecting the U.S. role in world affairs. Chapter Five explores the degree to which budget pressures may be limiting the domestic investments necessary to maintain U.S. international influence. Chapter Six concludes with some speculation about things that might have happened if the U.S. fiscal situation had been more robust and comments on approaches to fiscal consolidation that preserve U.S. international influence.

CHAPTER TWO

# A Brief History of U.S. Public Finances

The basic facts about the emergence since 2001 of high levels (by historical standards) of U.S. government debt are generally well known. Nonetheless, a brief review of some salient points may provide a helpful introduction to the discussion that follows dealing with the possible consequences of this debt.

## The Recent Rise of U.S. Government Debt

Figure 2.1 traces the history of U.S. federal outlays and receipts since the end of World War II. Federal receipts began to fall in FY 2001, first as a result of a mild recession and then as a consequence of substantial income tax reductions (the so-called Bush-era tax cuts) enacted in

**Figure 2.1**
**U.S. Federal Receipts and Outlays, by Fiscal Year**

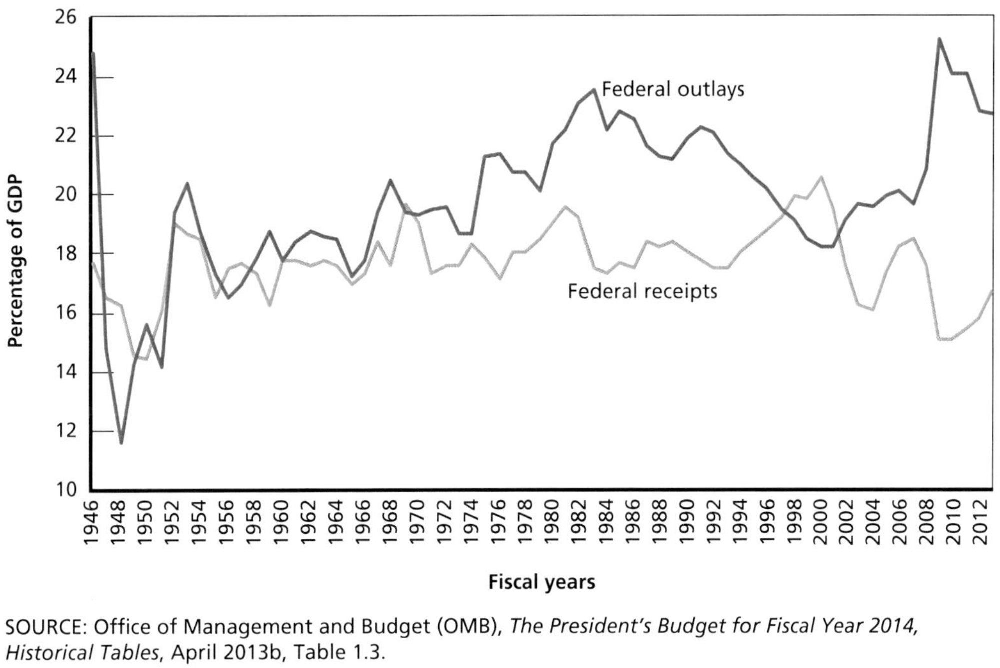


SOURCE: Office of Management and Budget (OMB), *The President's Budget for Fiscal Year 2014, Historical Tables*, April 2013b, Table 1.3.

RAND *RR353-2.1*

2001 and 2003.[1] Receipts increased again from FY 2004 through FY 2007 as a result of strong economic growth but collapsed with the onset of the global financial crisis and the consequent Great Recession in FY 2008.

Federal outlays began to rise after FY 2001 with growing expenditures for the Global War on Terror and conflicts in Iraq and Afghanistan. Outlays grew rapidly from FY 2007 through FY 2009 with the large stimulus programs aimed at stabilizing the economy during the Great Recession and the intensification of the conflicts in Iraq (the "troop surge") and Afghanistan. Outlays declined again as a percentage of GDP after FY 2009. This decline was due to the expiration or phasing down of stimulus programs put in place to combat the recession, the beginning of the drawdown of military forces in Iraq and Afghanistan, and growing GDP. The federal budget moved from a surplus equivalent to 2.4 percent of GDP in FY 2000 to a deficit of 10.1 percent of GDP in FY 2009, the largest deficit, as a share of GDP, since 1945 (see Figure 2.2).

The large federal deficits after FY 2000 drove levels of outstanding government debt—both general and federal[2]—to levels, as a percentage of GDP, not seen since the end of World

**Figure 2.2**
**U.S. Federal Budget Balance, by Fiscal Year**

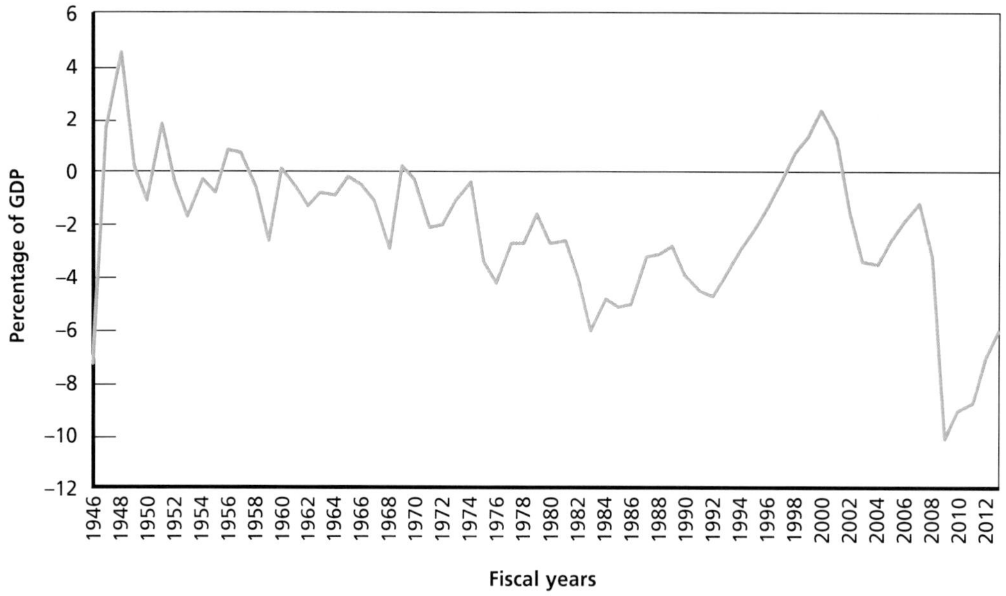


SOURCE: OMB, 2013b, Table 1.3.
RAND *RR353-2.2*

---

[1] These tax cuts were initially enacted in the Economic Growth and Tax Relief Reconciliation Act of 2001 (P.L. 107-16). The Jobs and Growth Tax Relief Reconciliation Act of 2003 (P.L. 108-27) accelerated the phasing in of these cuts.

[2] Gross federal debt held by the public is the usual "headline" figure for the debt of the U.S. federal government. It includes all outstanding debt of the federal government minus the debt that is held by federal government trust funds, such as the Social Security Trust Fund, the Medicare Trust Fund, and the Highway Trust Fund. Holdings of U.S. Treasury securities by the Federal Reserve System are included in debt held by the public. General government debt includes the outstanding debt of the federal government (including debt held by government trust funds) and the debts of state and municipal governments. This is the concept of government debt usually preferred for international comparisons, since the division of fiscal responsibilities and debt between central and local governments differs from one country to another.

War II (see Figure 2.3). In May 2013, the Congressional Budget Office (CBO) projected that, even after the tax increases enacted at the beginning of 2013 and with the full spending reductions mandated in the Budget Control Act—both the initial cuts that took effect in FY 2012 and the subsequent sequester—the long-term outlook is that federal debt held by the public, as a percentage of GDP, will remain near the levels recorded at the end of FY 2012.[3] After rising through FY 2014, the debt will decline modestly as a share of GDP through 2018. But without further reductions in spending or increases in federal revenues, the debt burden will begin to rise again as an aging population brings higher costs for Social Security and Medicare. As painful and politically contentious as recent tax increases and the spending reductions implemented as a result of the Budget Control Act have been, they do no more than stabilize the debt-to-GDP ratio at something close to current high levels. It is also important to note that the CBO projection is likely a lower bound for debt, because it depends on full implementation of the sequester. If Congress chooses to rescind the sequester or reduce its size, debt levels will be higher.

In April 2013, the IMF projected that U.S. general government debt will reach a peak as a share of GDP in 2014 and decline slightly through 2018.[4] (This projection takes into account the early 2013 tax increase and the spending reductions brought by the sequester.) The IMF projection does not extend far enough into the future to show the rise in debt after 2018 projected by CBO.

**Figure 2.3**
**U.S. Federal and General Government Debt, by Fiscal Year**

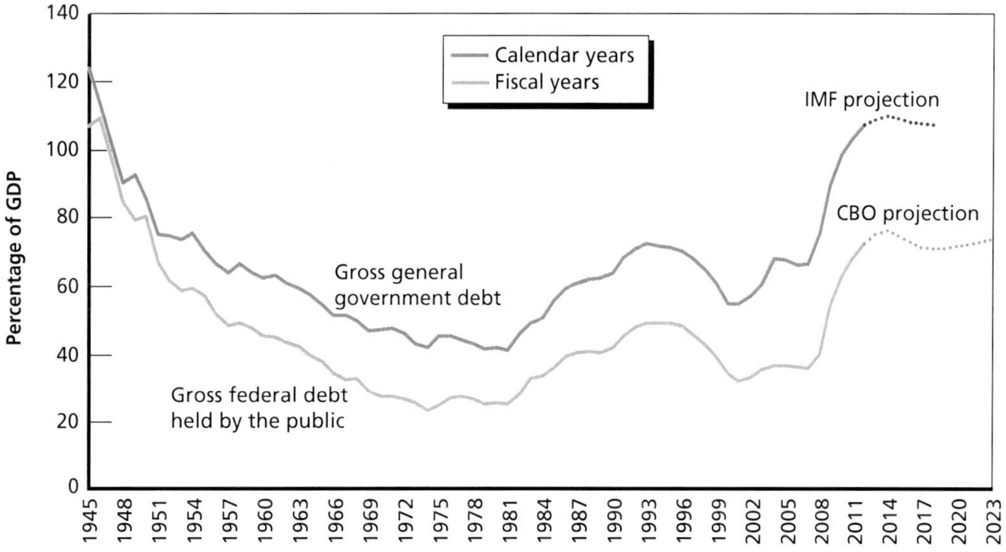


SOURCES: CBO, 2013; Federal Reserve System Board of Governors, "Flow of Funds Accounts of the United States: Historical Data," in *Release Z.1, Financial Accounts of the United States*, various dates; and IMF, 2013.
RAND *RR353-2.3*

---

[3] CBO, *Updated Budget Projections: Fiscal Years 2013 to 2023*, Washington, D.C., May 14, 2013.

[4] IMF, *Fiscal Monitor: Fiscal Adjustment in an Uncertain World*, April 2013.

Although the levels of federal debt held by the public and gross general government differ, both have shown the same general trajectory since 1945. Thus, for analytic purposes, the choice between one debt measure and the other is largely immaterial.

The bulk of the increases in federal outlays after FY 2007 came in the category of "programmatic mandatory outlays"—so-called entitlement programs, such as Medicare, Medicaid, and Social Security—although discretionary outlays—both defense and nondefense—also increased by smaller amounts (see Figure 2.4).[5] The President's budget submission for FY 2014 projects that discretionary spending will decline significantly after FY 2012, while spending on entitlements—unaffected by the Budget Control Act—will decline only marginally as a share of GDP.[6]

## Financing U.S. Government Debt

To date, the federal government has been able to finance its deficits on very favorable terms. The nominal interest rate on ten-year Treasury bonds, for example, was lower in the latter half of 2012 than at any time in the last 59 years (see Figure 2.5). The real interest rate on Treasury bonds was also very low—essentially zero (see Figure 2.6).

**Figure 2.4**
**Federal Outlays by Budget Function**

SOURCE: OMB, 2013b, Table 8.4
RAND *RR353-2.4*

---

5 OMB historical accounting does not provide figures for this categorization of federal outlays before 1962.

6 OMB, 2013b, Table 8.4.

**Figure 2.5**
**Nominal Yield on Ten-Year Constant-Maturity U.S. Treasury Bond**

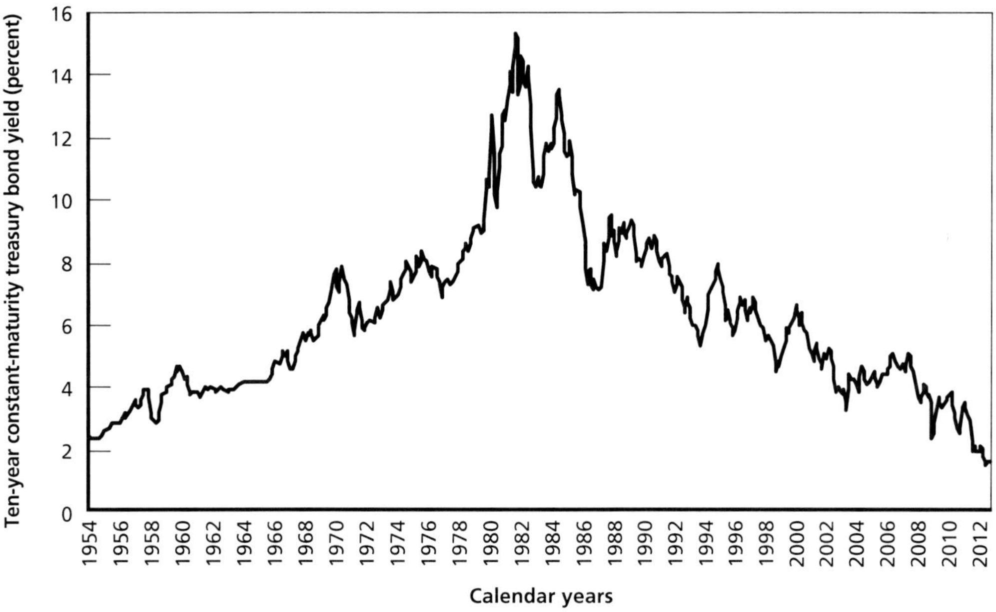


SOURCE: Federal Reserve System Board of Governors, *Release H.15, Selected Interest Rates: Historical Data*, various dates.
RAND *RR353-2.5*

**Figure 2.6**
**Real Yield on Ten-Year Constant-Maturity U.S. Treasury Bond**

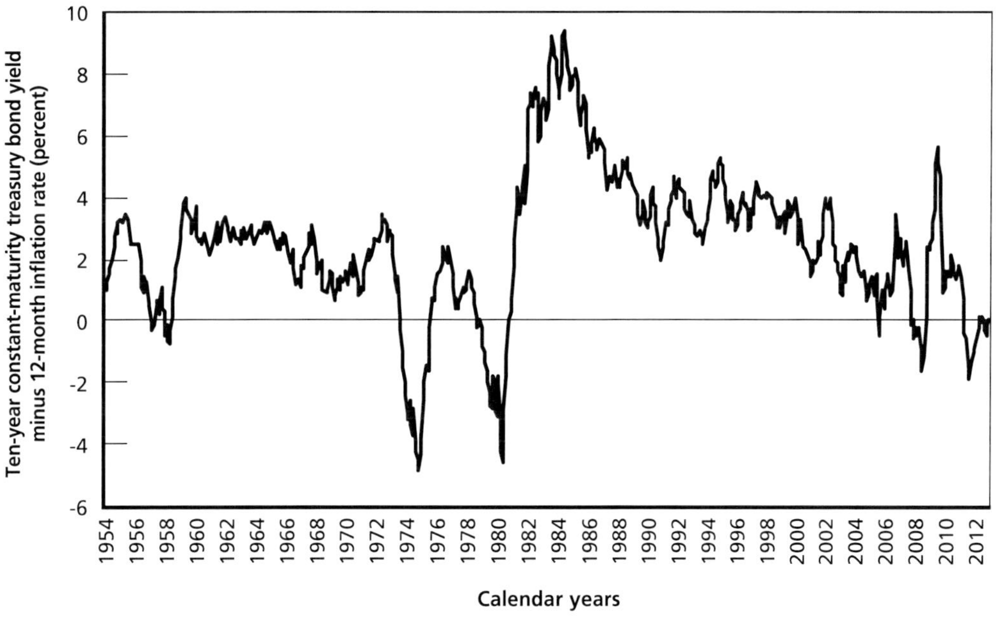


SOURCES: Federal Reserve System Board of Governors, *Release H.15,* various dates, and Bureau of Labor Statistics, "CPI for All Urban Consumers," database, undated.
RAND *RR353-2.6*

Of course, the past few years have not been ordinary times in financial markets. With short-term interest rates already near zero, the Federal Reserve launched a concerted effort to stimulate aggregate demand in December 2008 through a program of quantitative easing.[7] A second round of quantitative easing (popularly called QE2) began in November 2010. In this round, the Federal Reserve specifically bought large quantities of longer-dated Treasury securities to push down longer-term interest rates. This was followed in September 2011 by Operation Twist, in which the Federal Reserve bought Treasury securities of six to 30 years maturity and sold shorter-dated securities in an effort to reduce long-term interest rates even further. A third round of quantitative easing (QE3) started in September 2012 and featured an open-ended commitment from the Federal Reserve to buy mortgage-backed securities until conditions in U.S. labor markets improved. And in December 2012, QE4 brought new Federal Reserve purchases of long-dated Treasury securities.

Reinforcing the Federal Reserve's efforts to hold down long-term dollar interest rates have been worries beginning in 2009 about the safety of government debt in other major economies, especially in Europe. As concern grew over prospects for maintaining the single European currency, investors fled from the debt of peripheral Eurozone governments, especially Greece, Ireland, Italy, Portugal, and Spain, and sought safe havens in U.S. and German government debt, further reducing borrowing costs for the U.S. government.

Although there are no signs that either the unconventional policies of the Federal Reserve (quantitative easing) or concerns over the sustainability of Eurozone debt will end soon, these both constitute—almost by definition—extraordinary circumstances that cannot persist indefinitely. At some unknown time in the future, the conditions that have artificially suppressed U.S. government borrowing costs will abate, and the costs of financing the large U.S. debt will rise.

History demonstrates that market sentiment regarding sovereign debt can change quickly. Figure 2.7, for example, shows the history since 2008 of interest rate spreads between German ten-year government bonds and similar bonds from Greece, Ireland, Italy, Portugal, and Spain. After tracking German interest rates closely for the years since creation of the euro, yields on the bonds of peripheral Eurozone members began to rise—at first gradually in 2009 and then dramatically in 2010. Little changed in the underlying fiscal circumstances of these countries in 2010. They had all seen high government deficits since the onset of the global financial crisis at the end of 2007. But only in 2010, it seems, did markets begin to recognize that these deficits were unsustainable, and only then did bond yields begin to rise.

Table 2.1 shows the major sources of financing for the U.S. federal deficits since 1990. (Data from the decade before the rapid rise in federal debt provide some historical context.) From 2002 through 2007, foreign entities and especially foreign official entities (foreign central banks and sovereign wealth funds) were the dominant purchasers of new U.S. Treasury securities. U.S. domestic purchasers played only a minor role. With the onset of the financial crisis in 2008, the pattern changed somewhat. As worries grew about sovereign debt from other countries, private entities—both domestic and foreign—sought safety in U.S. federal

---

[7] Typically, central banks seek to stabilize the economy by acting to influence short-term (often, overnight) interest rates. When these rates are near zero, as they have been for several years in the United States, the central bank can seek to provide macroeconomic stimulus by buying longer-term securities, pushing down longer-term interest rates and ideally stimulating borrowing and investment. A central bank's purchase of longer-term government or private securities has been termed *quantitative easing* and is generally considered an unconventional or extraordinary measure.

**Figure 2.7**
**Ten-Year Central Government Bond Yields, Selected Eurozone Countries**

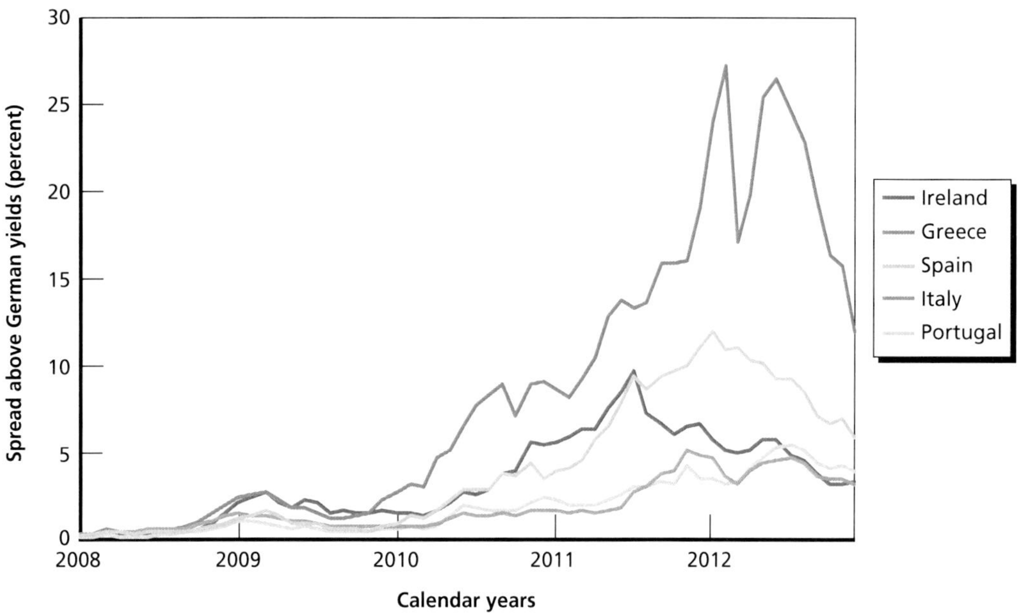


SOURCE: Eurostat, Interest Rates, "EMU Convergence Criterion Series—Monthly Data," data table, June 12, 2013.
RAND *RR353-2.7*

debt, although foreign official entities remained large net buyers of Treasury securities. From 2009 through 2011, the U.S. Federal Reserve was a large net purchaser of Treasury securities through its policy of quantitative easing. Especially in 2011, the Federal Reserve filled a gap left by the retreat of foreign and domestic purchasers from the market for U.S. securities. In 2012, however, the effect of Operation Twist became visible, as the Federal Reserve offset purchases of long-term treasury securities with the sale of short-term debt, reducing net purchases to near zero. In the Federal Reserve's absence, foreign and domestic buyers resumed large-scale purchases of Treasury securities.

During the period of rising U.S. federal debt—2002 through 2012—foreign entities purchased just over one-half (52 percent) of net new Treasury issues. Foreign official entities accounted for 37 percent of net new issues. Not surprisingly, the share of U.S. Treasury securities held by foreigners (as a share of all U.S. federal debt held by the public) rose from 30 percent at the end of 2001 to 49 percent at the end of 2012 (see Figure 2.8).[8]

Although it is true that the United States has been heavily dependent on foreigners as direct purchasers of federal debt during the last decade, this is not the entire story. The rightmost column in Table 2.1 shows the net inflow of foreign capital to all nonfederal U.S. entities. In 2009, 2010, and 2012, foreigners were net *sellers* of nonfederal U.S. assets. In effect, foreigners were financing part of their purchases of federal debt through sales of non-Treasury (mostly private-sector) assets. This was one aspect of a more general flight to quality, a reaction to uncertainty about the state of the broader U.S. economy during the financial crisis. The consequence of this shift in assets was that, while the U.S. federal government was becoming

---

8 The Treasury International Capital system provides estimates of foreign ownership back only as far as 2000.

**Table 2.1**
**Purchases of U.S. Treasury Securities ($B)**

| | | Purchased by | | | | | |
|---|---|---|---|---|---|---|---|
| | | Foreign Entities | | | | | |
| | | | Of which | | | | |
| Calendar Year | Net New Issues of Treasury Securities | Total | Official | Private | Federal Reserve | Other Domestic Purchasers | Net Foreign Lending Excluding Treasury Securities |
| 1990 | 239 | 27 | 30 | –3 | 8 | 204 | 24 |
| 1991 | 292 | 34 | 15 | 19 | 31 | 227 | 5 |
| 1992 | 304 | 56 | 19 | 37 | 29 | 219 | 39 |
| 1993 | 248 | 73 | 49 | 24 | 37 | 138 | 6 |
| 1994 | 156 | 65 | 31 | 34 | 33 | 58 | 58 |
| 1995 | 143 | 161 | 69 | 92 | 14 | –32 | –78 |
| 1996 | 147 | 263 | 116 | 147 | 13 | –129 | –128 |
| 1997 | 23 | 124 | –7 | 130 | 40 | –141 | 95 |
| 1998 | –55 | 19 | –10 | 29 | 21 | –95 | 48 |
| 1999 | –71 | –32 | 12 | –45 | 26 | –65 | 266 |
| 2000 | –295 | –75 | –5 | –70 | 34 | –254 | 553 |
| 2001 | –5 | 19 | 34 | –14 | 40 | –64 | 395 |
| 2002 | 257 | 161 | 61 | 100 | 78 | 18 | 339 |
| 2003 | 398 | 276 | 185 | 92 | 37 | 85 | 255 |
| 2004 | 363 | 367 | 273 | 94 | 51 | –55 | 168 |
| 2005 | 307 | 245 | 113 | 132 | 26 | 36 | 469 |
| 2006 | 184 | 150 | 209 | –58 | 35 | –1 | 657 |
| 2007 | 238 | 165 | 98 | 67 | –38 | 111 | 453 |
| 2008 | 1,239 | 712 | 549 | 163 | –265 | 792 | 25 |
| 2009 | 1,444 | 554 | 570 | –16 | 301 | 589 | –314 |
| 2010 | 1,580 | 740 | 442 | 298 | 245 | 595 | –357 |
| 2011 | 1,067 | 412 | 171 | 241 | 642 | 13 | 143 |
| 2012 | 1,141 | 474 | 339 | 136 | 3 | 664 | –100 |

SOURCE: Federal Reserve System Board of Governors, *Release Z.1,* various dates, Tables F.106 and F.209. Data used were current in May 2013.

more indebted to foreigners, the nonfederal sector was becoming less indebted. Indirectly, the nonfederal sector of the U.S. economy was making room for sharply increased federal borrowing. This is illustrated in Figure 2.9.

The basic national income accounting identity holds that government deficits plus private domestic investment must equal private saving plus foreign saving (that is, the inflow of foreign capital). Although net U.S. government borrowing rose from minus 1.5 percent of GDP in 2000 to 11.9 percent of GDP in 2009, the net inflow of foreign capital actually *fell* from 4.1 percent of GDP to 2.7 percent of GDP over the same period. The sharp increase in government borrowing had to be accommodated by increases in domestic saving and decreases in private domestic investment, as shown in Figure 2.9. From 2000 to 2009, gross private saving rose from 13.8 percent of GDP to 18.4 percent. Gross private domestic investment fell even more, from 17.8 percent of GDP to 10.9 percent. The discrepancy (except for a rounding error) is

**Figure 2.8**
**Foreign Holdings of U.S. Treasury Securities as a Share of Total Federal Debt Held by the Public**

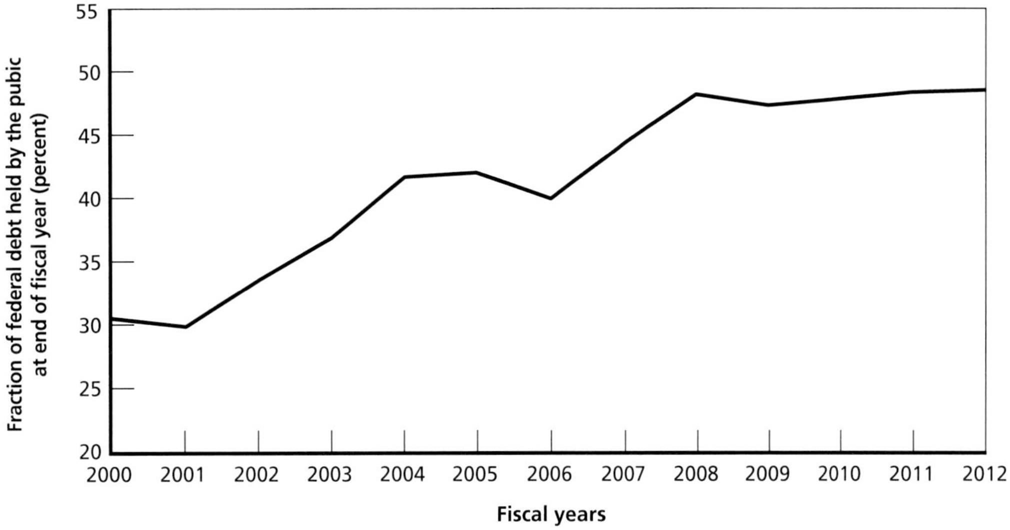


SOURCES: Total federal debt held by the public is from U.S. Department of the Treasury, *Monthly Statement of the Public Debt (MSPD) and Downloadable Files*, database, July 5, 2013. Estimated foreign holdings are from U.S. Department of the Treasury, "Major Foreign Holders of Treasury Securities," April 30, 2013.

RAND *RR353-2.8*

**Figure 2.9**
**Financing U.S. Federal Government Deficits**

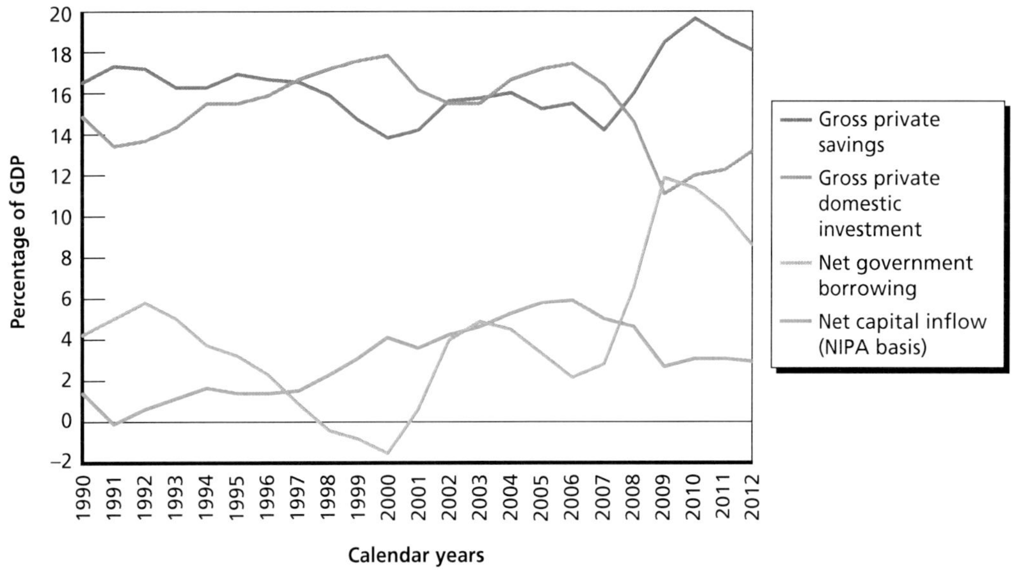


SOURCE: U.S. Department of Commerce, Bureau of Economic Analysis, *National Income and Product Accounts Tables*, webpage, May 2013, Tables 3.1 and 5.1.
NOTES: Figure reflects total government borrowing—federal, state, and local. NIPA = net income and product accounts.

RAND *RR353-2.9*

made up by a rise in purchases of Treasury securities by the Federal Reserve from 0.3 percent of GDP in 2000 to 2.2 percent in 2009 and a substantial increase in net government capital grants from minus 0.3 percent of GDP in 2000 to 1.0 percent in 2009. This increase in net capital transfers reflects large grants from the federal government to state and local governments as part of the fiscal stimulus program to combat the recession.

While heavy the federal government dependence on foreign lenders may be unnerving, it is probably not a major problem for the United States for the foreseeable future. The United States is able to raise foreign funding in its own currency, and thus, foreign debt does not expose the U.S. government to exchange-rate risk.

It would be unrealistic to attribute the rise of private saving and the fall in private investment during the first decade of this century entirely to the rise of federal debt. Certainly, the financial crisis and the ensuing recession prompted significant retrenchment on the part of the household and the corporate sectors, with consequences for saving and investment. We return in Chapter Five to possible links between government debt and investment. But whatever the cause, the most damaging legacy of the era of rising government debt will be the loss of productive private investment.

CHAPTER THREE

# Government Debt and U.S. Defense Spending

Until quite recently, large U.S. federal deficits and rapidly rising federal debt have not adversely affected U.S. defense spending or, presumably, U.S. military capabilities. Indeed, from FY 2000 through FY 2010, rising defense spending *contributed* to rising deficits and debt, although to a lesser extent than did spending on entitlement programs. During this period, defense outlays grew from 3.0 percent of GDP to 4.8 percent. In real (inflation-adjusted) terms, defense outlays increased 69 percent over the same period (see Figure 3.1).[1]

These increases included the costs of operations in Iraq and Afghanistan, and Figure 3.1 gives a somewhat exaggerated picture of both the rise (up to FY 2010) and the fall (after FY 2010) in defense spending. Overseas contingency operations (OCOs) accounted for much of the increase in defense outlays from FY 2000 through FY 2010, and the drawdown of U.S. forces in Iraq and Afghanistan accounts for about two-thirds of the reductions from FY 2010 through FY 2014. Reductions in the DoD base budget, which excludes OCO outlays, have

**Figure 3.1**
**Defense Outlays—FYs 1962 Through 2017**

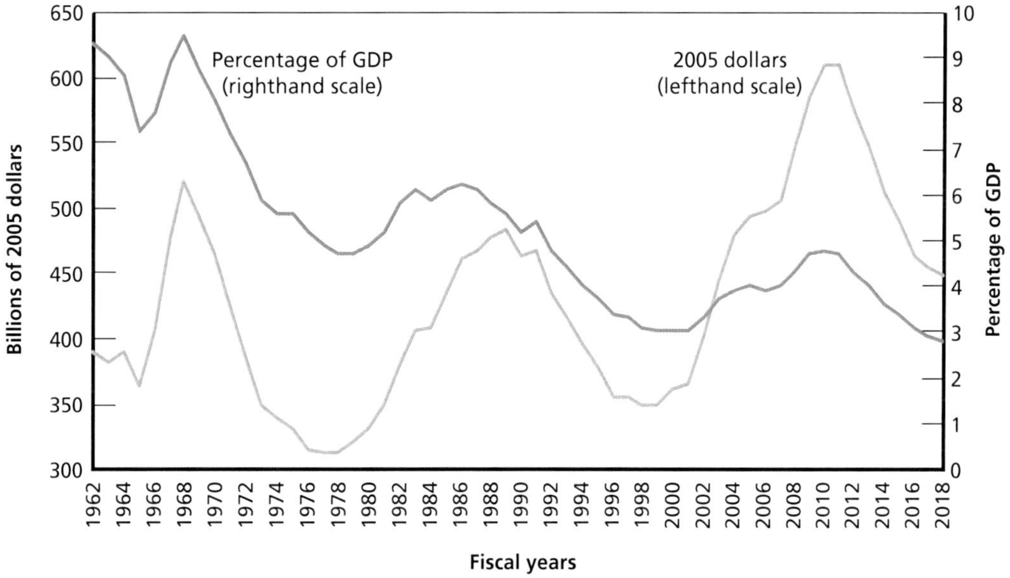


SOURCE: OMB, 2013b, Tables 8.2 and 8.4.
RAND *RR353-3.1*

---

[1] OMB reports outlays for this definition of defense spending back only to 1962.

been more modest (see Figure 3.2). But after FY 2014, OCO outlays will be minimal, and the full burden of further cuts will fall on the base budget. Without the costs of OCOs, "base" defense spending rose to 3.7 percent of GDP in FY 2010, and the increase in real terms from FY 2000 to FY 2010 was 29 percent.

Total defense outlays began to decline, both in real terms and as a share of GDP, after FY 2010, initially because the costs of operations in Iraq were abating. But starting in FY 2012, the provisions of the Budget Control Act began to affect defense spending directly, a trend that will continue for the next several years, unless the White House and Congress strike some budget deal. In March 2013, Congress approved and the President signed the Consolidated and Further Continuing Appropriations Act, 2013 (P.L. 113-6). This act included DoD's appropriation for FY 2013. This appropriation was consistent with the terms of the Budget Control Act and reflected the sequester that went into effect on March 1, 2013. The appropriations act cut DoD spending for FY 2103 dramatically—11 percent in nominal terms (12.8 percent in real terms) from the FY 2012 level. Whether any relief from the sequester will be granted and whether DoD will in fact have to absorb this very large cut remain to be seen.

DoD's budget request for FY 2014, presented to Congress in April 2013,[2] is considerably higher—by $52 billion dollars in FY 2014—than what would be permitted if the sequester remains unchanged.[3] (Figure 3.1 reflects projections in the President's budget and does not show the sharp reduction—possibly temporary—in defense outlays in FY 2013 as a result of the sequester.) As Under Secretary of Defense (Comptroller) Robert Hale explained, the

**Figure 3.2**
**DoD Total and Base Budget Authority**

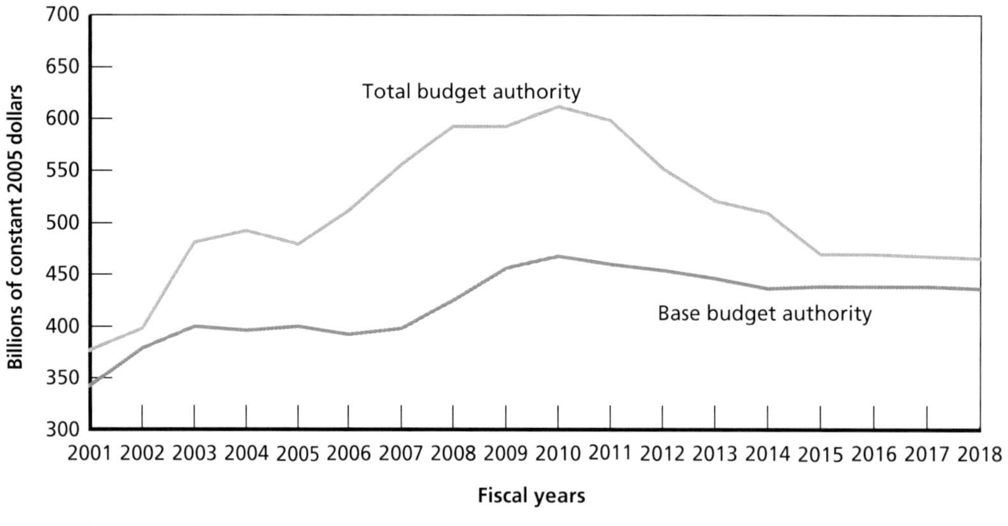


SOURCES: DoD, *FY 2014 Green Book*, May 2013; U.S. Department of Defense, Office of the Under Secretary of Defense (Comptroller), April 2013a, p. 9; and OMB, 2013b, Table 10.1.
NOTE: This figure shows base budget authority and total budget authority back only to FY 2001 because the concept of the base budget did not exist before then.
RAND *RR353-3.2*

[2] An overview of the DoD budget request for FY 2014 is available, in the form of briefing charts, on the website of the Office of the Under Secretary of Defense (Comptroller). See U.S. Department of Defense, Office of the Under Secretary of Defense (Comptroller), *Fiscal Year 2014 Budget Request and FY 2013 Update*, April 2013a.

[3] DoD, Office of the Under Secretary of Defense (Comptroller), 2013b.

President's overall budget proposal achieves the ten-year deficit reduction targets the Budget Control Act set and therefore may provide a basis for Congress to "detrigger" the sequester.[4] This would allow the higher levels of defense spending proposed in the DoD budget request.

The FY 2014 budget request projects that, after peaking in FY 2010 at 4.8 percent of GDP, total defense outlays will fall to 2.8 percent of GDP in FY 2018, their lowest level by this measure since before World War II. But because GDP has grown, defense outlays in constant dollars, although much lower than at their peak level in FY 2010, will remain well above the lows recorded in FY 1978 and FY 1999. Significantly, the President's budget projects defense spending to stay *above* its pre-9/11 level in real terms. That is, the President's budget proposes less than a full return to the level of defense spending that characterized the last period during which the U.S. military was not engaged in major overseas operations. As Figure 3.2 illustrates, the projected base budget remains well above its FY 2001 level. These projections, however, must be viewed as upper bounds for defense spending, possible only if the sequester is rescinded or modified.

Because the DoD FY 2014 budget request assumes elimination of the sequester requirement for equal percentage cuts to all budget lines, it proposes quite different trajectories for outlays under each of the major defense budget titles in the years going forward (see Figure 3.3). Military compensation is exempt from the spending cuts the Budget Control Act mandated, and outlays for military personnel show the smallest percentage decline in outlays from FY 2010 through FY 2018—14 percent in real terms, to be accomplished through reductions in the size of the military force. Although only a small part of the total budget, outlays for military construction will see the sharpest decline (63 percent). Among military departments, the Army will see the biggest reductions in outlays, down almost 50 percent in real terms from FY 2010 through FY 2018. This is more a reflection of the winding down of conflicts in Iraq and Afghanistan than an obvious reaction to budget constraints. The Navy (including the Marine Corps) would see a real reduction of 14 percent and the Air Force 15 percent.[5]

The number of military personnel will also be coming down. The FY 2013 Future Years Defense Program (FYDP) projected active-duty military end-strength to contract by 7.2 percent from FY 2012 to FY 2017 (see Figure 3.4).[6] Reserve and National Guard forces (not shown in the figure) are projected to shrink by 2.6 percent from FY 2012 to FY 2017. As with total outlays, this is a much smaller reduction in active-duty personnel than the one that occurred from the mid-1980s through the mid-1990s as the Cold War was coming to an end. As with total outlays, this reduction principally reflects the declining need for military personnel with the end of overseas combat operations and as a result of restructuring to make use of more-capable weapon platforms that accomplish particular missions with reduced manpower. Unlike total outlays, active-duty end strength will fall below pre-9/11 levels, but because the military is becoming less manpower intensive, this does not necessarily imply a less-capable force. We do not know the consequences for numbers of military personnel if the budget sequester provisions remain in effect beyond FY 2013. As with total outlays, these projections of active-duty end strength must be viewed as a best-case scenario.

---

[4] DoD, Office of the Under Secretary of Defense (Comptroller), 2013b.

[5] DoD, 2013, Table 6-13.

[6] The FY 2014 FYDP is not yet available.

**Figure 3.3**
**Defense Outlays in Constant Dollars, by Major Budget Title**

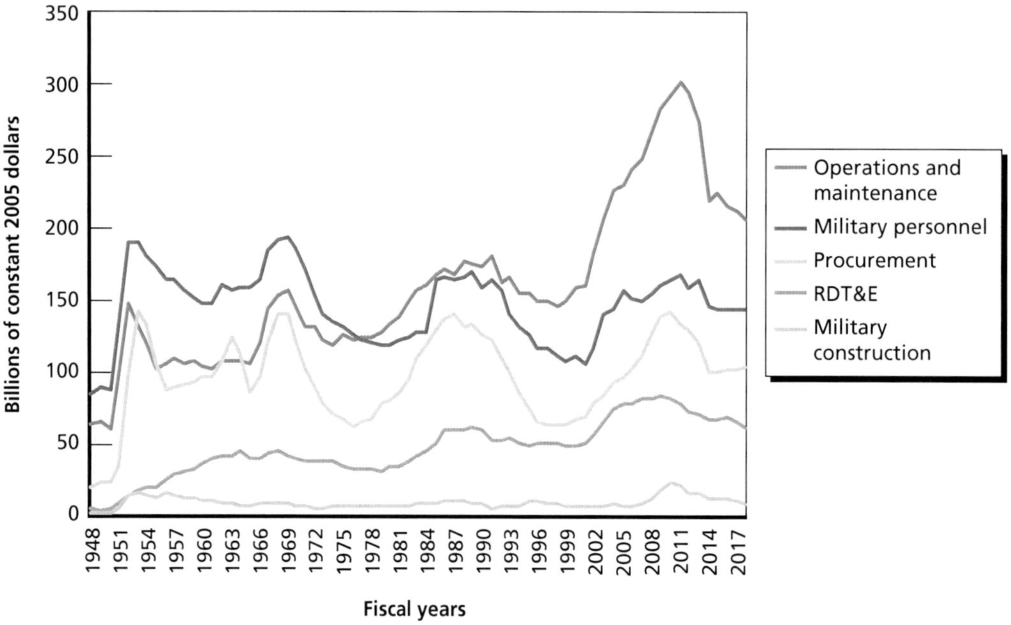


SOURCE: DoD, 2013.
RAND *RR353-3.3*

**Figure 3.4**
**Active-Duty Military End Strength**

SOURCE: U.S. Department of Defense, Statistical Information Analysis Division, *DoD Personnel and Procurement Statistics*, website, various dates.
RAND *RR353-3.4*

Although some reductions in military compensation and benefits are projected, the DoD FY 2013 Budget Request noted that these will be "disproportionately small."[7] The FY 2014 budget request is consistent with this policy. Individual service members will not bear the burden of reduced defense spending.

The FY 2013 budget request also proposed terminating or significantly restructuring a number of high-profile defense acquisition programs. Among the programs affected are the Global Hawk Block 30 drone, the Joint Strike Fighter, the Ground Combat Vehicle Program, the *Ohio*-class nuclear submarine replacement, and shipbuilding more generally.

It is beyond the scope of this analysis to assess the magnitude of new risks that the United States may face as a consequence of defense spending reductions. Neither do we attempt to establish whether there would in fact be any new risks; it is possible that reduced levels of spending will suffice to ensure U.S. national security.

Even the first round of cuts the Budget Control Act required were sufficiently large, however, to have prompted DoD to revise its overall military strategy, consistent with having fewer resources than the department had previously anticipated. In January 2012, DoD issued new high-level strategic guidance to serve as the basis for force planning in coming years.[8] The document repeatedly emphasizes that the need to reduce overall outlays strongly influenced the new guidance. In the first paragraph of his accompanying letter, President Barack Obama specifically acknowledged that fact: "The Budget Control Act of 2011 mandates reductions in federal spending, including defense spending." In the concluding paragraph of the same letter, the President notes that "[t]he fiscal choices we face are difficult." The introduction to the guidance itself states that it reflects "an assessment of the U.S. defense strategy in light of the changing geopolitical environment and our changing fiscal circumstances." The conclusion reiterates that "[t]he balance between available resources and our security needs has never been more delicate."

The strategic guidance clearly envisions a U.S. military that is smaller and less capable than in the past. In his covering letter, Defense Secretary Leon Panetta says that "[t]he Joint Force of the future . . . will be smaller and leaner." This smaller and leaner force will have narrower missions than in the past. For example: "Even when U.S. forces are committed to a large-scale operation in one region, they will be capable of denying the objectives of—or imposing unacceptable costs on—an opportunistic aggressor in a second region." This contrasts with the "two major wars" planning objective of earlier years.[9] The guidance goes on to state that "U.S. forces will no longer be sized to conduct large-scale, prolonged stability operations." Presumably, this means no more operations of the sort that are now ending in Iraq and Afghanistan. U.S. forces will still be capable of maintaining "a sustainable pace of presence operations abroad, including rotational deployments and bilateral and multilateral training exercises. . . . However, with reduced resources, thoughtful choices will need to be made regarding the location and the frequency of these operations." Finally, the guidance explicitly recognizes future constraints on U.S. military capabilities: "We are determined to maintain a ready and capable force, even as we reduce our overall capacity."

---

[7] DoD, Office of the Under Secretary of Defense (Comptroller), *Fiscal Year 2013 Budget Request,* February 2012, p. 17.

[8] DoD, *Sustaining U.S. Global Leadership: Priorities for 21st Century Defense*, January 2012.

[9] Whether U.S. forces were actually capable of winning two simultaneous major wars is a matter of controversy, now of largely historical interest. Perhaps the new objective does not amount to much of a change.

The changed strategy reflected only the first round of defense budget reductions that the Budget Control Act specifies. Now, a second round of spending cuts—in excess of $500 billion (about 10 percent of projected spending) over ten years for DoD—has been triggered. Whether these cuts will be fully implemented over the full period the Budget Control Act covers—through FY 2021—is unknown.

Assessing the military and foreign policy consequences of these cuts, if in fact they are implemented, is beyond the scope of this report. Others have considered this matter, however, and opinion is divided about the consequences of full implementation of the sequester. In 2012, Defense Secretary Leon Panetta predicted that this second round of cuts would be "disastrous" for U.S. defense capabilities.[10] Some respected defense analysts seem generally to agree with him, although they use less colorful language in expressing their views. A few months before Panetta's statement, for example, David Barno and Nora Bensahel of the Center for New American Security wrote: "We judge the U.S. military's ability to execute America's global engagement strategy, as it is currently articulated, will be placed at high risk if total national defense cuts exceed $500 billion to 550 billion over ten years." They go on to note that "if implemented fully over the next decade, the [Budget Control Act's] spending caps and automatic spending reduction process could cut national defense spending by up to $1 trillion"—well in excess of the $500 billion to 550 billion that they judge will place U.S. strategy at "high risk."[11]

In a similar vein, Michael O'Hanlon of the Brookings Institution wrote: "It is possible to imagine additional defense cuts in weapons, force structure, and other expenses of up to $200 billion over a decade, above and beyond those now scheduled [before the sequester]. These savings, however, would be considerably less than envisioned under sequestration."[12] He goes on to say that defense spending cuts "foreseen by either sequestration or plans like that of the Simpson-Bowles commission, which while hardly emasculating the country or its armed forces, would be too risky for the world in which we now live."

But there are dissenters from the view that the cuts the Budget Control Act and subsequent sequestration require will expose the United States to significant new risks. In November 2012, for example, the Defense Advisory Committee, a group of military and foreign policy experts convened by Stimson found that "by implementing the new strategy [i.e., the strategy outlined in *Sustaining U.S. Global Leadership*] the US can defend and promote its interests with varying, but no more than moderate, risks" in a spending scenario "that would result if the sequester provision of the [Budget Control Act] were implemented" and indeed in a scenario with defense cuts half again as large.[13]

---

[10] Donna Cassata, "Panetta Warns of 'Disaster' from Defense Cuts", *Associated Press*, June 13, 2012.

[11] David W. Barno, Nora Bensahel, and Travis Sharp, *Hard Choices: Responsible Defense in an Age of Austerity*, Center for a New American Security, October 2011, pp. 5–6.

[12] Michael O'Hanlon, *A Moderate Plan for Additional Defense Budget Cuts*, Washington, D.C: The Brookings Institution, February 2013, p. iii.

[13] Defense Advisory Committee, *A New U.S. Defense Strategy for a New Era: Military Superiority, Agility, and Efficiency*, Stimson, November 2012, p. 6.

CHAPTER FOUR

# Fiscal Performance and the Economic Instruments of International Influence

This chapter takes up the question of whether poor fiscal performance in recent years may be affecting the ability of the United States to exert influence internationally or to shape global events through economic means. The exercise of economic power can be active—when, for example, the U.S. government assists allies or imposes economic sanctions against adversaries. Other examples of active economic power include influencing the operations of international institutions or shaping the rules of international commerce, finance, and environmental protection. Active economic power can be deployed to encourage or discourage foreign entities from taking particular actions or to modify the behavior of foreign companies that seek access to U.S. markets or resources. Economic power can also operate passively or incidentally, as when U.S. citizens, companies, or institutions spread American norms, practices, attitudes, or values abroad by example or by association with foreign actors. Whether active or passive, economic power must be based on substantial engagement in international affairs; consequently, it makes sense to ask whether deficits and debt render the United States and its institutions less central or less consequential in key areas of international activity that plausibly contribute to making the world more congenial to U.S. interests and values.

## Debt and Economic Growth

The most fundamental basis for economic power is simply the size of a nation's economy. A larger economy generates more resources to shape world affairs—militarily or otherwise. Because it constitutes a larger share of key international activities, a larger economy is, almost by definition, more consequential in global affairs.

Standard Keynesian theory argues that government deficits can replace temporarily flagging private demand and thus stabilize output and incomes during a recession. The effectiveness of Keynesian stimulus remains contentious. But there is general agreement that any positive effects of fiscal stimulus are temporary at best: Keynesian-style stimulus cannot produce long-term economic growth.

Economists are only beginning to explore—theoretically and empirically—the long-term consequences for economic growth of persistent deficits and the debt that they leave behind. A recent working paper from the Bank for International Settlements provides a good summary of the current state of knowledge about the real effects of debt.[1] The basic conclusion is that, in

[1] Cecchetti, Mohanty, and Zampolli, 2011.

moderation, debt—government, corporate, or household—is beneficial. Debt allows smoothing of consumption in the face of inevitable income shocks, finances investment, provides opportunities for relatively low-risk earnings, and creates liquidity that makes credit markets more efficient. Evidence is accumulating, however, that, above certain thresholds, debt constitutes a drag on economic growth. The mechanisms for this are not yet well understood, but a number of hypotheses can be advanced:

- In some circumstances, government credit demand crowds out productive domestic investment.
- The uncertainty inherent in an unsustainable fiscal situation inhibits private investment.
- The noncontingent nature of debt creates leverage that in turn increases volatility, magnifying the consequences of inevitable positive or negative shocks to an economy. Risk-averse investors will invest less in a volatile environment.
- High debt constrains the ability of governments—either for financial or political reasons—to pursue stimulative fiscal policies in an economic downturn.[2]

A number of recent studies have found that, for industrialized countries, the negative effects of debt increase rapidly when gross general government debt crosses a threshold of between 80 or 90 percent of GDP.[3] Examining 26 episodes of government-debt "overhang" in advanced economies—government debt above 90 percent of GDP for five or more consecutive years—Reinhart, Reinhart, and Rogoff found that real GDP growth is reduced by about 1 percent per year until government debt is brought below the 90-percent threshold.[4] Using data from a panel of 18 Organization for Economic Cooperation and Development (OECD) countries (including the United States) from 1980 through 2006, Cecchetti, Mohanty, and Zampolli estimated that an additional 10 percentage points of gross general government debt (as a percent of GDP) above a threshold of about 85 percent of GDP reduces the average growth rate of real per capita GDP by about 13 basis points (hundredths of a percentage point) during the next five years.[5] This is about double the effect for additional debt below the threshold of 85 percent.[6]

Applying Cecchetti, Mohanty, and Zampolli's result to the United States, we undertook the following thought experiment: Compare two cases. In the first case, the level of gross general government debt remains at its 2001 level of 54.7 percent of GDP. This was the level just before the most recent run-up of government debt. In the second case, the level of gross general debt is as it actually was from 2001 through 2012 and continues to grow between 2012

---

2 Another BIS working paper that finds evidence that industries that rely heavily on outside finance or hold fewer tangible assets tend to grow faster in OECD countries that implement more countercyclical fiscal policies. See Philippe Aghion, David Hemous, and Enisse Kharroubi, *Cyclical Fiscal Policy, Credit Constraints, and Industry Growth*, Basel, Switzerland: Bank for International Settlements, working paper 340, February 2011.

3 Cecchetti, Mohanty, and Zampolli, 2011; Reinhart and Rogoff, 2009; Reinhart and Rogoff, 2010; Reinhart, Reinhart, and Rogoff, 2012; and Kumar and Woo, 2010. Footnote 5 in Chapter One discusses current controversy about Reinhart and Rogoff, 2010 . The other citations in this footnote appear to remain unchallenged.

4 Reinhart, Reinhart, and Rogoff, 2012.

5 Cecchetti, Mohanty, and Zampolli, 2011.

6 The countries in Cecchetti, Mohanty, and Zampolli's panel are all developed economies that are able to borrow in their own currencies. Although Cecchetti and his coauthors do not test the proposition explicitly, exchange rate volatility presumably does not contribute significantly to this finding.

**A Troubling Anecdote: International Monetary Fund New Arrangements to Borrow**

A current anecdote illustrates how U.S. fiscal difficulties and the political stalemate over how to deal with them are hindering U.S. international leadership and influence.

To combat financial instability resulting from the "Asian financial crisis" (which affected countries well beyond Asia), the IMF in 1997 established a new mechanism through which it could increase the resources at its disposal by borrowing from its member countries. These New Arrangements to Borrow (NAB) took the form of member states pledging to provide credit to the fund in certain circumstances. The United States was among the member states that made such pledges.

In 2009, in the depths of the recent global financial crisis, the IMF sought to expand the resources available through the NAB. A number of member states, again including the United States, made additional contingent pledges of credit.

In April 2012, facing the possible need to support struggling European governments and banking systems, the IMF called once again for an expansion of the NAB. As of this writing (May 2013), 39 member countries had pledged additional resources. In this round, however, the United States is conspicuous by its absence from the group of pledging member countries. This absence is particularly striking because countries that are plausible rivals to the United States for influence in international affairs have made pledges—China, Russia, Brazil, Korea, Japan, Germany, France, the United Kingdom (UK), and Saudi Arabia. Even countries in more precarious fiscal circumstances than the United States have pledged resources—Spain and Italy.[a]

The U.S. government has offered no formal explanation of its failure to pledge resources in the most recent expansion of the NAB. Objections on policy grounds seem unlikely because previous contributions suggest at least general U.S. support for these financing arrangements. For the United States, however, pledges of even contingent financial support require congressional approval, and the U.S. administration has not requested the necessary approval. At a time when painful tax increases and/or reductions in government spending for domestic programs are required, it is perhaps not surprising that the administration is reluctant to ask for authority to increase support for an international institution. The present paralysis over U.S. budget policy renders the situation yet more difficult.[b] It is not hard to imagine that, with less-pressing fiscal needs at home, the United States would have contributed to the expansion of the NAB. As matters stand, the United States seems to have missed an opportunity to exercise leadership on an issue of international significance. So far, it has missed an opportunity even to follow.

---

[a] IMF, "IMF Managing Director Christine Lagarde Welcomes Additional Pledges to Increase IMF Resources, Bringing Total Commitments to US$456 Billion," press release, No. 12/231, June 19, 2012, and IMF, "IMF Managing Director Christine Lagarde Welcomes Pledges from Algeria and Brunei Darussalam to Boost Fund Resources," press release, No. 12/388, October 13, 2012.

[b] The extent of budget-related difficulties is further illustrated by proposals relating to the most recent increase in the U.S. quota in the IMF (the basic commitment to the IMF). The President's budget for FY 2014 proposes that the increase in the U.S. quota agreed to at the G-20 meeting of 2010 be offset by "an equivalent rollback in U.S. participation in the IMF's NAB for no change in the overall U.S. financial participation in the IMF." See OMB, *Budget of the United States, Fiscal Year 2014*, April 2013a, p. 875. The participation in the NAB referred to in the FY 2014 President's budget is the commitment made in response to the 2009 expansion of the credit facility. Not only has the United States chosen not to participate in the most recent call for NAB commitments, the FY 2014 budget proposes to reduce the previous NAB commitment to fund the increase in the U.S. IMF quota.

and 2018, as projected by the IMF in April 2013.[7] How much lower would real GDP be in the second case compared with the first? In 2012, the implied difference is small—only about 1 percent. This is because the United States crossed the 85-percent-of-GDP threshold only in 2009, and the long-term negative effects of high debt levels would be just beginning to bite. Extending the projection out into the future, however, suggests that by 2019, high debt levels will have cost the United States some *4 percent of real GDP*.

Considerable caution should be attached to such projections. Cecchetti, Mohanty, and Zampolli's estimates are based on a panel of OECD countries, and it is possible that the United States is not typical of this panel. To test this, we estimated an equation similar to Cecchetti, Mohanty, and Zampolli's for the United States only and over a longer period—1960 through 2007.[8] (To use Cecchetti, Mohanty, and Zampolli's formulation,[9] we needed GDP data for five years beyond the last debt observation. Thus, our most recent debt observation is 2007, before the United States crossed the "high debt" threshold.) Our results were inconclusive.[10] Perhaps this means that the negative effects of high debt do not apply to the United States. But perhaps it simply reflects the fact that U.S. experience with high debt levels is very recent; we do not have observations above the debt threshold that other studies suggest is critical. This inconclusive result provides no basis for complacency.

More generally, the possible relationship between government debt and future growth remains controversial. Certainly, growth and debt are simultaneously determined, with each affecting the other. The persistence of high-debt episodes even after recessions have passed, however, suggests that debt "overhangs" are not simply the consequences of business-cycle recessions. (For further discussion of this issue, see Chapter Five.)

Certainly, how government spending is deployed will also affect future growth. Government outlays for needed infrastructure, for education, or for R&D, for example, will presumably promote future growth. Government outlays for income support or other sorts of redistribution will have less-positive long-term effects. Also, government spending or tax policies that distort the structure of the economy through subsidies for uncompetitive industries or by encouraging unproductive or unsustainable investment in, say, residential housing can do long-term harm. The emerging evidence suggests that, averaging across countries and across periods, higher levels of government debt in developed economies are associated with slower future growth. As Chapter Two noted, the expansion of the U.S. federal debt was accompanied

[7] IMF, April 2013.

[8] We are not aware of other studies that explore the effect of government debt on future GDP growth specifically for the United States.

[9] Cecchetti, Mohanty, and Zampolli, 2011, pp. 11–12.

[10] Specifically, we estimated an equation for the United States similar to the equation Cecchetti, Mohanty, and Zampolli estimated for a panel of OECD countries. Using annual data from 1960 through 2007, we regressed the five-year growth rate of GDP (the five years following the last observation of the independent variables) on the ratio of gross general government debt to GDP, the rate of population growth, the rate of inflation, the dependency ratio, net private investment as a share of GDP, research and development (R&D) expenditures as a share of GDP, the ratio of liquid liabilities of the banking system to GDP (as a measure of financial integration), and a business-cycle indicator. We excluded a number of variables that Cecchetti, Mohanty, and Zampolli included to differentiate across countries in their panel (not relevant in a regression for a single country). We initially included a number of additional variables from Cecchetti, Mohanty, and Zampolli's estimation but ultimately excluded them because they contributed nothing to the explanatory power of the regression. Like Cecchetti, Mohanty, and Zampolli, we found small negative effects of debt on future growth. Unlike them, our estimates of the effects of debt on growth are not statistically significant. Because we have no observations for debt levels above thresholds cited by the literature, we could not test for nonlinear responses above a particular threshold.

by significant increases in spending for entitlements and military operations, purposes without obvious links to productivity gains and future economic growth.

If Cecchetti, Mohanty, and Zampolli's findings do, in fact, apply to the United States, slowing economic growth will reinforce a trend that has been apparent for some time. The U.S. share of global output held more or less steady at between 22 and 23 percent for two-and-a-half decades from 1980 through 2005 (see Figure 4.1).[11] The temporary rise above 23 percent—in 1998 through 2000—reflects rapid growth during the technology boom. Since 2005, however, this share has declined markedly, falling to 18.6 percent in 2011. The shares of traditional U.S. allies—the European Union (EU) and Japan—have been in (apparently secular) decline for longer periods. China and, to a lesser extent, India and Russia have gained shares during the period of U.S. decline. Growth in China and India has been the result of significant domestic economic reforms. Russia's growth may owe more to strong energy prices than to successful structural reform.

The growth of other economies is not entirely negative for the United States. Indeed, these emerging markets constitute new sources of demand for U.S. exports. But as a matter of algebraic necessity, the shares of global output that other countries account for have to decline to accommodate the rising shares of emerging markets, and it is *relative* GDP that is most plausibly associated with international influence. The experience of the late 1990s, moreover, suggests that the U.S. economy *can* gain share even when China, India, and Russia are also gaining share. Whatever the causes of the recently declining U.S. share of world output,

**Figure 4.1**
**Shares of Global GDP at Purchasing Power Parity Exchange Rates**

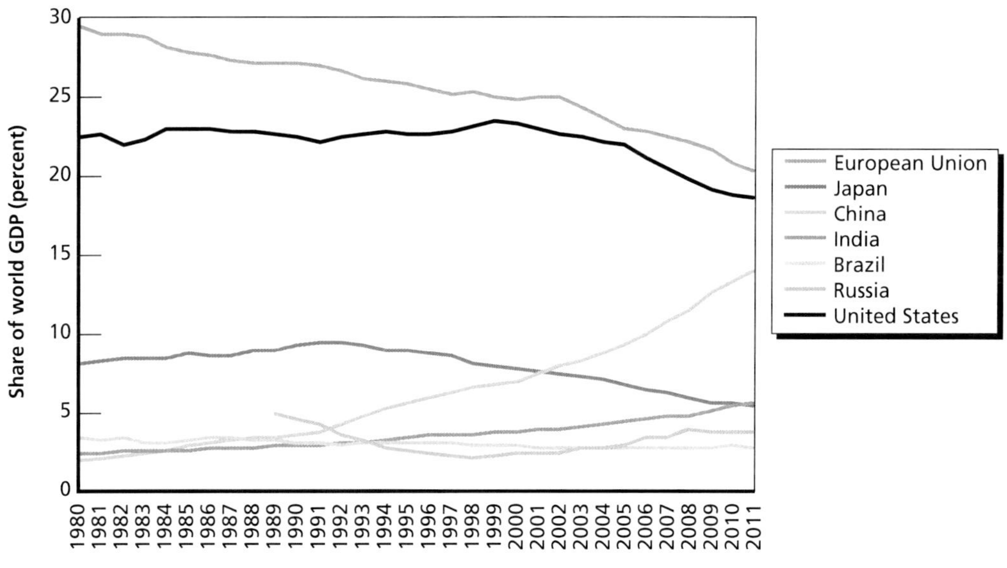


SOURCE: International Bank for Reconstruction and Development, 2013.
RAND *RR353-4.1*

[11] The World Bank has been calculating purchasing-power-parity shares of GDP only since 1980.

however, compounding this decline with the consequences of high government debt cannot enhance U.S. international influence.

## Economic Policy Uncertainty and Economic Growth

Recent U.S. history has been characterized not just by rising government debt but also by rising *uncertainty* about the future of economic policy as Congress and the White House struggle over how to put federal finances on a sustainable basis. Both the popular and the financial press report constantly on the supposed negative consequences of this uncertainty: Firms are reluctant to hire additional workers without clear knowledge of their future tax liabilities or a reasonable forecast of future aggregate demand; businesses accumulate cash rather than undertake productive investments in plants and equipment; households pay down debt and defer major purchases; etc. These behaviors plausibly combine to slow economic growth and recovery from the recent recession.

Recently, researchers at Stanford University and the University of Chicago devised an index of policy-related economic uncertainty in the United States.[12] The index seeks to distinguish between general economic uncertainty and uncertainty about economic policy. It has three components: the frequency of references in news media to economic policy uncertainty, the number of federal tax code provisions set to expire in coming years, and the dispersion of forecasts of inflation and federal government outlays. The future of U.S. government outlays is particularly uncertain in the current environment.

Figure 4.2 plots the evolution of the index from 1985 (when it began) through 2012, showing a distinct increase in policy uncertainty since 2007. The maximum value of the index was in August 2011, at the time of the confrontation between the White House and congressional Republicans over the federal debt ceiling. (That confrontation was resolved with the Budget Control Act of 2011.)

Baker, Bloom, and Daly presented some evidence that their index is not just an academic curiosity.[13] Although causality is typically murky, movements in the index seem to foreshadow real economic developments. For example, the authors estimate that an increase in the index equal to that recorded from 2006 through 2011 is associated with a decline in real GDP of 2.2 percent after four quarters. Further, the reduction in real GDP persists for at least two years after that.[14] Thus, it is possible that some of the weakening in real U.S. GDP growth—at least

---

[12] Scott R. Baker, Nicholas Bloom, and Steven J. Daly, *Measuring Economic Policy Uncertainty*, Economic Policy Uncertainty website, working paper, April 2013.

[13] Baker, Bloom, and Daly, 2012.

[14] Formally, Baker and his coauthors estimated a vector autoregression (VAR) model using quarterly data from 1985 through 2011. The variables included in the VAR were the uncertainty index, the Standard and Poors 500 index (as a measure of investor confidence), the federal funds rate, employment, private investment, consumption, and GDP. The impulse response function resulting from the VAR shows a maximum decline of GDP after four quarters, which attenuates only modestly over the following two years. Attributing causality in VAR schemes is always problematic, and the finding that a rise in policy uncertainty equal to the increase from 2006 through 2011 is necessarily an out-of-sample projection. Additional analyses the authors reported demonstrate that separating the effect of policy uncertainty from the effect of overall investor confidence is difficult. Nonetheless, the negative association between policy uncertainty and future GDP growth appears to be robust within the analyses that are reported. In any event, it is hard to argue that uncertainty about future economic policy is good for economic growth. See Baker, Bloom, and Daly, 2012.

**Figure 4.2**
**Monthly Index of U.S. Economic Policy Uncertainty**

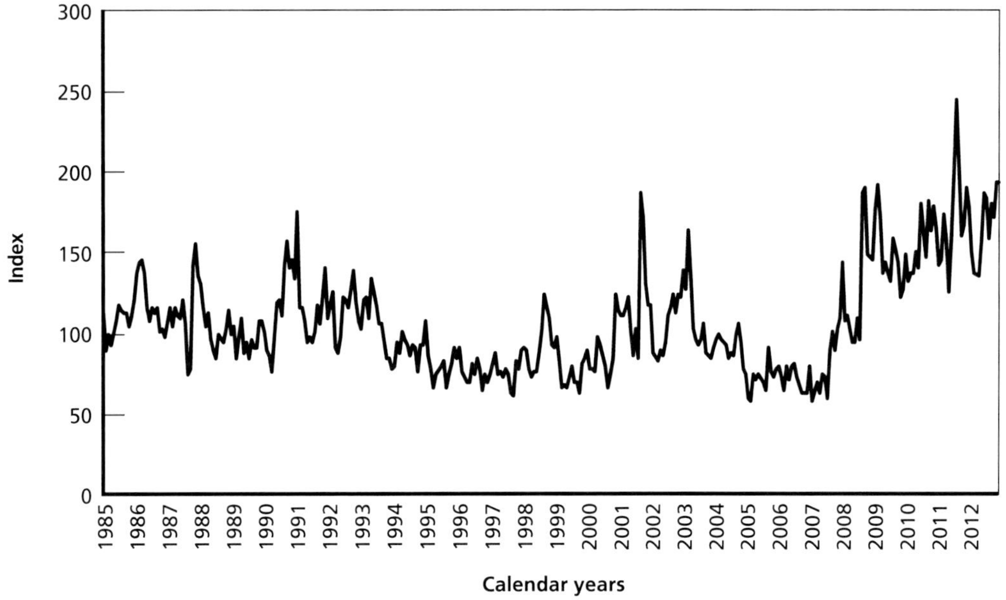


SOURCE: Economic Policy Uncertainty, "U.S. Monthly Index," database, various dates.
RAND *RR353-4.2*

in the most recent years—is due to uncertainty about economic policy. Without question, the inability of Congress and the President to agree on measures to limit federal deficits and debt has contributed to this policy uncertainty.

## Debt and Trade

If government debt does have a negative effect on economic growth, debt may also indirectly contribute to reduced U.S. presence in other arenas key to exercising economic power. Consider, for example, the U.S. role in world trade. With a substantial presence in the world trading system, the United States can exercise influence in establishing international trading rules. Other nations may think twice before adopting trade policies that run counter to U.S. interests for fear of having their access to the large U.S. market curtailed. Active engagement in international trade also supports the presence abroad of U.S. firms or their representatives, and this presence provides opportunities to spread American values and practices.

Figure 4.3 shows that U.S. shares of global merchandise and commercial services trade (imports plus exports) have tracked the U.S. share of global output closely since the mid-1980s and that U.S. trade shares have fallen as the U.S. share of world output fell. No doubt, other

---

A more recent paper examining the effect of uncertainty about the economic situation (as opposed to uncertainty about future economic policy) reaches a similar conclusion: Rudiger Bachman, Steffen Elstner, and Eric Sims, "Uncertainty and Economic Activity: Evidence from Business Survey Data," *American Economic Journal: Macroeconomics*, April 2013, pp. 217–249. Using dispersion in survey responses about the future economic situation as a measure of uncertainty, its authors found that, in the United States, a rise in uncertainty is associated with a significant and persistent reduction in economic activity.

**Figure 4.3**
**U.S. Shares of World Trade and World Output**

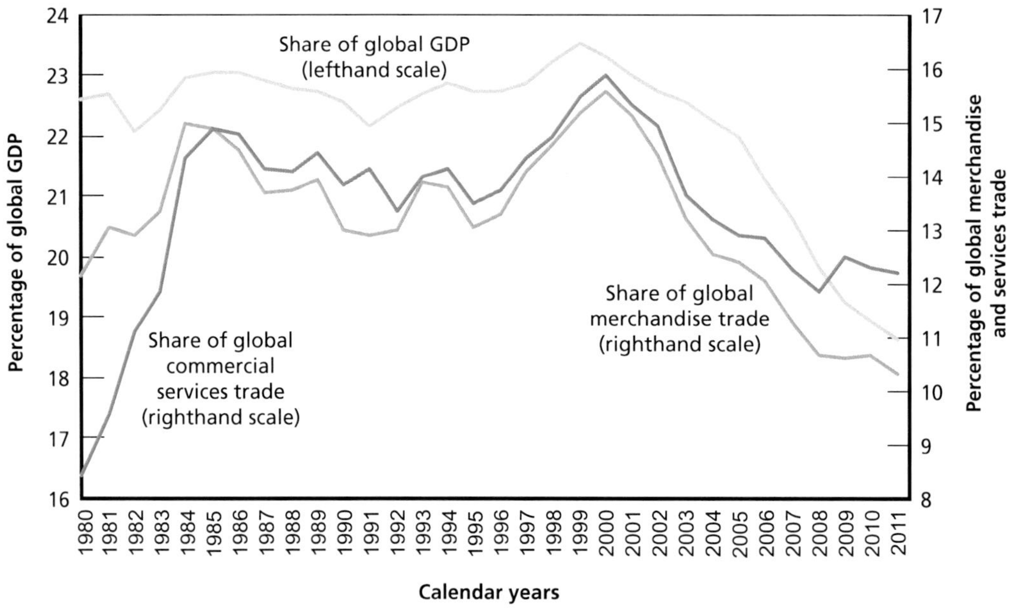


SOURCE: International Bank for Reconstruction and Development, 2013.
RAND *RR353-4.3*

factors, such as the changing composition of world trade,[15] have affected U.S. trade shares, but the correlation with the U.S. share of global output remains striking. To the extent that high deficits and debt and policy uncertainty will depress future U.S. real GDP, they will also likely depress the U.S. role in world trade.

## Voting Rights in International Organizations

One consequence of declining shares of world output and trade (and therefore a potential indirect consequence of high government debt) is declining voting power in important international financial institutions, such as the IMF and the World Bank. Among the factors that go into the formula that the IMF uses to calculate national quotas in the fund, and therefore voting shares, are shares of world GDP and shares of total international payments for merchandise trade, services trade, income on investments, and transfers. The World Bank uses the IMF quotas as its basis for allocating shares in the bank and therefore voting power in it. Thus, a declining share of world output and cross-border commercial or financial activity leads to a declining voice in how these important organizations operate.

Voting shares in the major international financial organizations are adjusted irregularly. Table 4.1 shows the declining U.S. voting share in three of these institutions—the IMF, the World Bank, and the Asian Development Bank—since 1996. (This is the period for which voting shares are conveniently available for all three institutions.)

---

[15] See, for example, Benjamin R. Mandel, "Why Is the U.S. Share of World Merchandise Exports Shrinking?" *Current Issues in Economics and Finance*, Vol. 18, No. 1, 2012.

**Table 4.1**
**U.S. Voting Shares in Major International Financial Institutions (percent)**

| Year | IMF | World Bank | Asian Development Bank |
|---|---|---|---|
| 1996 | 17.78 | 17.20 | 13.20 |
| 2000 | 17.35 | 16.49 | 13.05 |
| 2011 | 16.80 | 16.05 | 12.82 |

SOURCES: Annual reports of the IMF, the World Bank, and the Asian Development Bank, respectively, for the years shown in the table.

## Debt and the Dollar

Figure 4.4 shows the evolution of the value of the dollar on a price-adjusted basis against the currencies of a "broad" (as defined by the Federal Reserve) group of major U.S. trading partners.[16] This index peaked in February 2002, shortly after U.S. federal debt began its recent rise, and has been generally declining since. The coincidence in timing is striking, but it is hard to draw any clear causal link between growing U.S. government debt and the value of the dollar. A falling currency can be an indicator that investors are losing confidence in the government or monetary authority of the issuing country. It can just as well, however, be a consequence of relative monetary policies and interest rates in different countries. Given the very aggressive efforts of the U.S. Federal Reserve in the last five years to force down interest rates, it would be hard to argue that the dollar's recent weakness reflects anything more than low dollar interest rates. More to our point, it is hard to see any particular link between the value of the dollar per se and U.S. international influence.

Neither is a dollar that is stronger or weaker inherently good or bad for the broad U.S. economy. A strong dollar generally harms producers, who have a harder time selling in foreign markets or competing with lower-priced imports. But simultaneously, a stronger dollar benefits consumers, because imports are cheaper, and domestic producers have less scope to raise prices in the face of more-competitive imports. There is no reason to see one of these effects as more important or beneficial than the other for the overall economy.

A more relevant consideration from the standpoint of U.S. economic influence has to do with the role the dollar plays in the international financial system. The dollar's position as the world's principal reserve currency, for example, serves U.S. national interests by creating a source of demand for the currency and the associated opportunities for seigniorage.[17] Control over the international reserve currency also gives U.S. monetary authorities some ability to shape global monetary conditions. Similarly, the dollar's dominant position in foreign exchange markets confers an advantage on individuals and firms for whom the dollar is the natural transaction currency: Most foreign exchange transactions can be completed with only

[16] The Federal Reserve has calculated this index since 1973, following the final collapse of the Bretton Woods system of fixed exchange rates.

[17] *Seigniorage* refers to the profit that accrues to an issuing authority as a result of issuing coins or currency. It is the difference between the face value of a coin or note and the cost of making and issuing that coin or note.

**Figure 4.4**
**Price-Adjusted Value of the Dollar Against Currencies of Major U.S. Trading Partners**

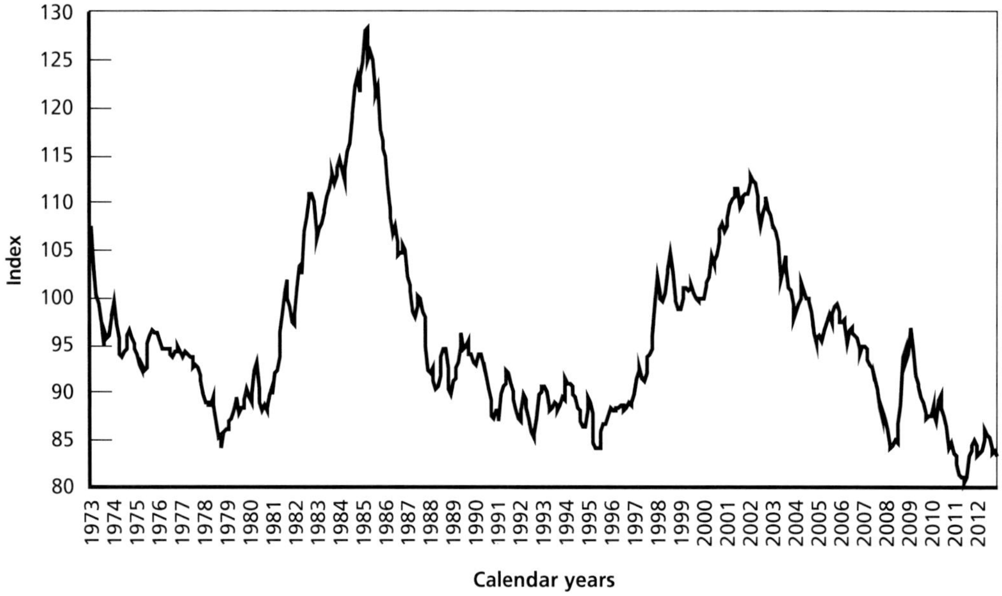


SOURCE: Federal Reserve System Board of Governors, "Price-Adjusted Broad Dollar Index—Monthly Index," in *Foreign Exchange Rates—H.10*, historical data, July 1, 2013.
RAND *RR353-4.4*

one trade. For other parties, two transactions will sometimes be required—one into dollars and then another into the desired destination currency.

In neither of these respects, however, does there appear to be significant erosion of the dollar's position since the onset of U.S. fiscal problems. Although the euro has gained share at the expense of the dollar since it was introduced in 1999, the dollar retains its position as dominant international reserve currency (see Figure 4.5).[18]

The dollar also maintains a dominant position in foreign exchange markets. In 2010, the triennial BIS survey of foreign exchange transactions found that the dollar figured in 84.9 percent of all foreign exchange transactions (see Figure 4.6).[19] This was far ahead of its nearest rival, the euro (39.1 percent), although it was modestly down from the 89.9 percent registered in 2001, the first survey to include the euro. This may reflect the shrinking U.S. role in world trade or perhaps increased opportunities to carry out trades directly between nondollar currencies.

[18] Data on the currency composition of official foreign exchange reserve holdings come from the IMF's Currency Composition of Official Foreign Exchange Reserves reports. Unfortunately, some countries—especially "Emerging and Developing Economies" (in the IMF's definition)—report the total value of their reserves but not their currency composition. Notably, China does not report the currency composition of its reserve holdings. Among "Advanced Economies," reporting on currency composition of reserves is quite high; in 2011, only 11 percent of Advanced Economy reserves were "unallocated" by currency. In contrast, 61 percent of Emerging and Developing Economies (a category that includes China) reserves were unallocated. Consequently, Figure 4.5 shows the currency shares of reserves for Advanced Economies only. The figure shows the share of total reserves, both allocated to a specific currency and unallocated. Composition of Official Foreign Exchange Reserves data are available only for 1995 forward.

[19] BIS, *Triennial Survey of Foreign Exchange and Derivatives Market Activity in 2010—Final Results,* Basel, Switzerland, December 1, 2010. By definition, each foreign exchange transaction involves two currencies. Consequently, the sum of all currency shares in such a transaction must be equal to 200 percent.

**Figure 4.5**
**Shares of Total Advanced-Economy Official Foreign Exchange Reserves for Major Currencies at Yearend**

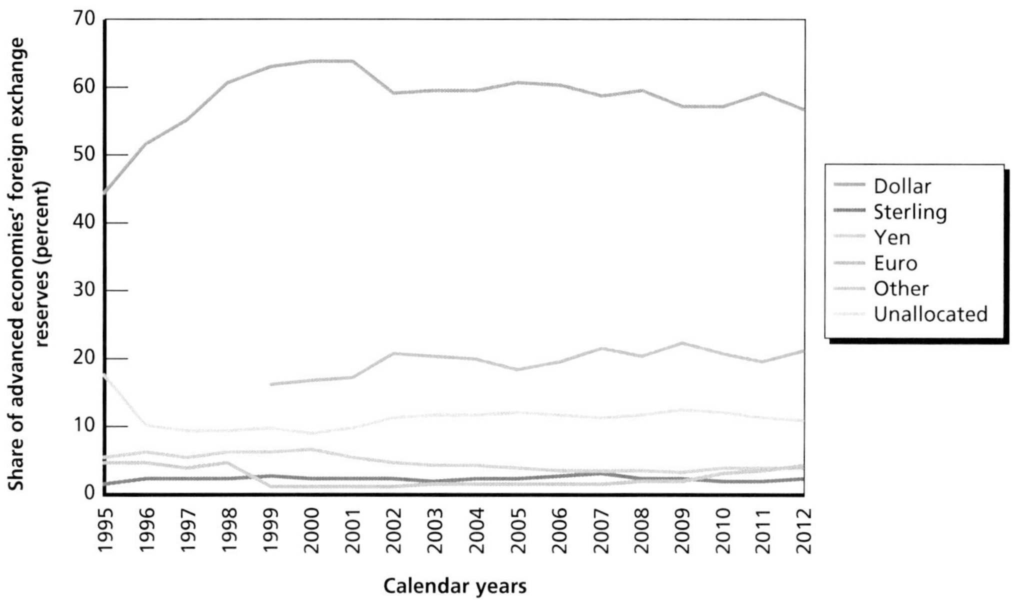


SOURCE: IMF, "Currency Composition of Official Foreign Exchange Reserves (COFER)," database, March 29, 2013.
RAND *RR353-4.5*

**Figure 4.6**
**Currency Shares of Foreign Exchange Transactions**

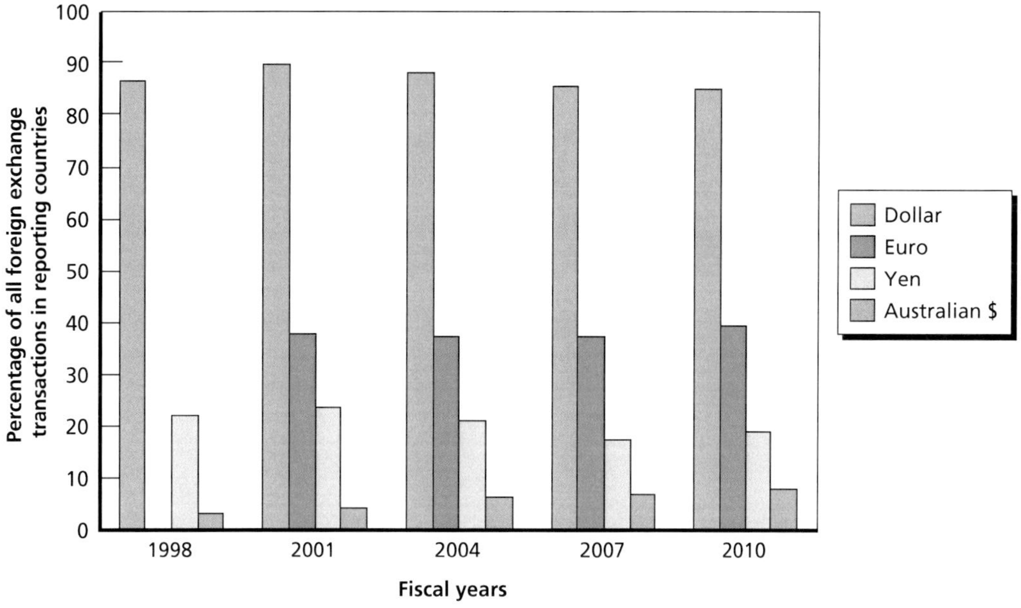


SOURCE: Bank for International Settlements, 2010.
RAND *RR353-4.6*

Interestingly, a recent working paper from the Peterson Institute of International Economics presents evidence that the renminbi has become the "reference currency"—the currency that other currencies most closely track—for East Asia.[20] The authors note that, since the renminbi began floating (at least partially) in 2010, "East Asia is now a renminbi bloc because the currencies of seven out of ten countries in the region—South Korea, Indonesia, Taiwan, the Philippines, Malaysia, Singapore, and Thailand—track the renminbi more closely than the U.S. dollar." This development likely reflects China's growing role in Asian regional trade, rather than any erosion in confidence in the dollar.

International banking constitutes another useful channel for exercising U.S. economic influence. Foreign customers of U.S. banks have to abide by U.S. rules for disclosure of information, and the transactions of U.S.-based banks are subject to monitoring and regulation from U.S. authorities. This oversight of banking transactions can be a tool for preventing money laundering and for enforcing certain kinds of financial and commercial sanctions. Fortunately, large U.S. deficits and debt do not appear to have diminished the U.S. position as a provider of international banking services. If anything, the U.S. position has strengthened in the past dozen years.

Traditionally, banks in the UK have been the preferred destination for individuals and companies wishing to hold deposits abroad. For as long as the BIS has been collecting information about cross-border deposits, UK banks have accounted for the largest share of these deposits, with the United States in second place. These relative positions remain unchanged. Since the late 1990s, banks in both the UK and the United States have been gaining shares at the expense of banks in Germany, Japan, and Hong Kong. Since 2008, the United States has also been gaining shares at the expense of the UK and Ireland (see Figure 4.7).[21] The failures of bank management and bank regulation that sparked the global financial crisis were not confined to the United States, and, if anything, international depositors seem to have deemed U.S. banks more-attractive destinations for deposits than banks elsewhere. Concern about European banks has apparently driven some depositors to seek safe havens in U.S. banks. This is almost certainly the explanation for the sharp drop in Ireland's share of deposits at the end of 2010. Although the UK is not part of the Eurozone, skittishness about UK banks and their exposure to European sovereign debt may have driven some deposits out of the UK.

## Spending to Support U.S. Representation Abroad

The U.S. federal government makes outlays for multiple nonmilitary programs aimed at representing the United States abroad or providing assistance to foreign countries. These outlays are grouped in the international affairs budget function, which includes international development and humanitarian assistance, international security assistance, the conduct of foreign policy,

---

[20] Arvind Subramanian and Martin Kessler, *The Renminbi Bloc Is Here: Asia Down, Rest of the World to Go?* Peterson Institute of International Economics, Working Paper 12-19, October 2012.

[21] The BIS continues to expand its reporting area—the countries whose banks report cross-border assets and liabilities. To create a more or less comparable base across years, we calculated each country's cross-border deposits as a fraction of such deposits held by banks in 16 countries that have been part of the BIS reporting area in all years shown in the figure. These countries are Belgium, Canada, Switzerland, Germany, Spain, France, the UK, Hong Kong, Ireland, Italy, Japan, the Cayman Islands, Luxembourg, the Netherlands, Singapore, and the United States. At the end of the second quarter of 2012, these 16 countries accounted for 87 percent of all cross-border deposits reported to the BIS.

**Figure 4.7**
**Shares of Cross-Border Bank Deposits Held in 16 Major Markets**

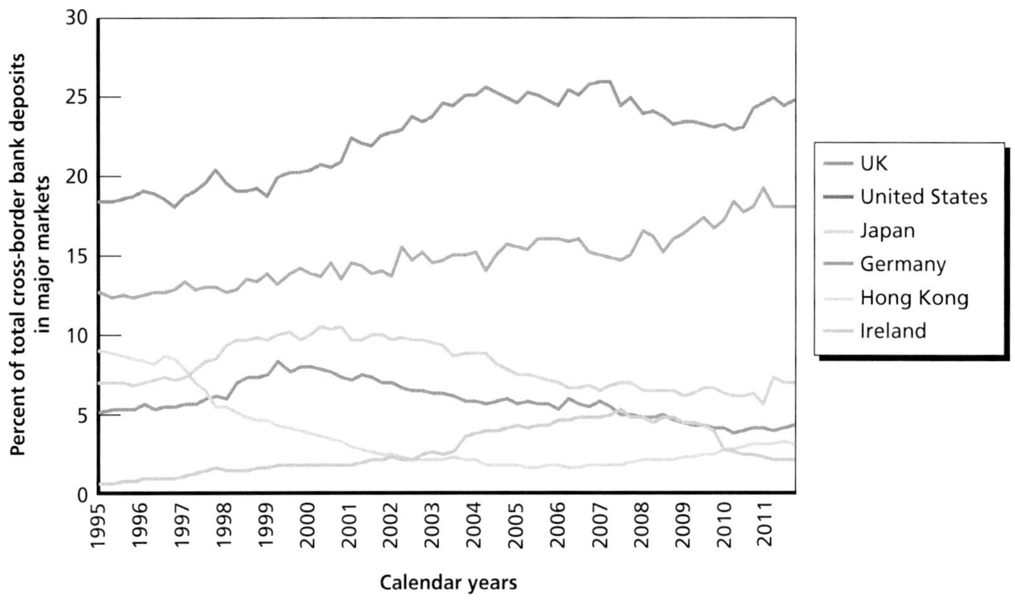


SOURCE: Bank for International Settlements, "Locational Banking Statistics," web page, June 3, 2013.
RAND *RR353-4.7*

foreign information and exchange activities, and international financial programs (support for the World Bank, the IMF, and other international financial institutions). Figure 4.8 shows the history of federal outlays for these purposes since the early 1950s, both as a share of GDP and in constant dollars. In constant-dollar terms, outlays for international affairs fluctuated around $20 billion 2005 dollars from the early 1960s through FY 2000. After that, outlays for these purposes rose rapidly, principally as a result of increased security assistance and development assistance to Iraq, Afghanistan, and (especially after FY 2008) Pakistan. Assistance to Israel also increased significantly after FY 2008. Far from being constrained by rising federal deficits and debt, expenditures for international affairs—mostly security assistance and development assistance—contributed to both deficits and debt from FY 2001 through FY 2012. In April 2014, OMB projected that outlays for international affairs would continue to grow through FY 2013 but decline after that, consistent with budget-cutting provisions of the Budget Control Act and the subsequent sequester.

U.S. assistance to some politically important countries in the Middle East and South Asia has suffered during the period of rising U.S. government debt, but it is hard to tie these reductions in assistance directly to the U.S. fiscal situation. In constant-dollar terms, for example, U.S. assistance to Egypt declined by 43 percent from FYs 2000 to 2013.[22] Declining assistance to Egypt cannot be strengthening U.S. influence in that country at a time when the situation

[22] This figure and the figures that follow in this paragraph are drawn from annual Congressional Budget justifications from the U.S. Department of State, which are available on the department's website. They include all assistance programs the Department of State and the U.S. Agency for International Development manage. These outlays are not identical to the outlays OMB reports in Budget Subfunction 151 (International Development and Humanitarian Assistance) and Budget Subfunction 152 (International Security Assistance). But in most recent years, the Department of State and U.S. Agency for

**Figure 4.8**
**Outlays for the International Affairs Budget Function, by Fiscal Year**

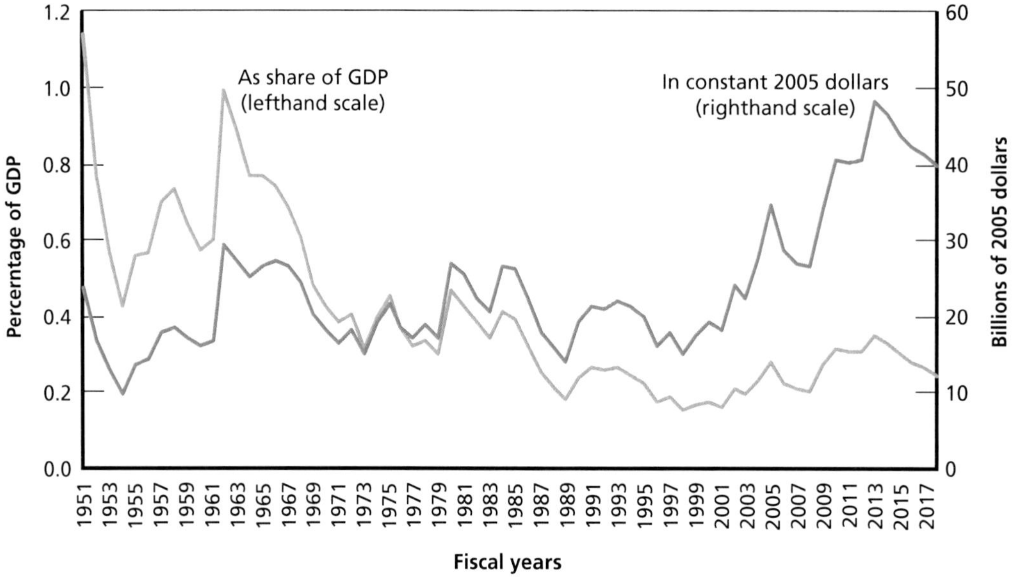


SOURCE: OMB, 2013b, Table 3.1.
RAND *RR353-4.8*

there is very fluid. But policy differences between the U.S. government and both the old and the new regimes in Egypt are sufficient to account for reduced levels of U.S. support, and there seems no particular reason to associate these reductions with budgetary constraints the U.S. government faces, particularly during a period when total foreign assistance has been rising.

Aid to Afghanistan has also fallen sharply in the most recent years, down 42 percent in constant-dollar terms from FY 2010 to FY 2013. Again, however, this probably reflects the changing nature of U.S. involvement in that country rather than direct budgetary pressure. Other significant reductions in assistance in recent years have affected Jordan (down 34 percent in real terms from FY 2008 to FY 2013) and Pakistan (down 10 percent in constant-dollar terms from FY 2009 to FY 2013).

## Conclusion

What emerges from the above considerations is a mixed picture of how U.S. fiscal disarray may be affecting the levers of U.S. international influence. The anecdote of U.S. nonparticipation in the latest round of commitments to the IMF's NAB is troubling and seems directly linked to the U.S. fiscal situation and to the political paralysis surrounding it. Other studies suggest that government debt at the current U.S. levels and uncertainty about future economic policy can slow economic growth. These effects, if they materialize, will further depress the U.S. share of global GDP, which has been declining since a year before the U.S. fiscal position began to deteriorate. The U.S. share of global trade has been declining even more markedly than the

International Development programs account for more than 90 percent of these budget subfunctions. At the time of this writing (May 2013), the Department of State budget justification for FY 2014 was not yet available.

U.S. share of global output, and declining U.S. growth as a result of high government debt will presumably result in a further decline in the U.S. trade share. The price-adjusted exchange value of the dollar has been declining since the U.S. fiscal position began to deteriorate, but this is likely due to very aggressive actions the Federal Reserve has taken to constrain dollar interest rates rather than to the fiscal situation of the U.S. government. The dollar remains the world's dominant reserve currency by a wide margin. Similarly, the dollar retains its position as the dominant transaction currency in foreign exchange markets. Foreign depositors are not fleeing U.S. banks. Federal spending in the International Affairs budget function has held up well since the onset of U.S. fiscal difficulties, but administration out-year projections suggest future curtailment of such spending.

CHAPTER FIVE

# Debt and Keeping the Nation Strong

In this chapter, we consider whether high federal deficits and debt may be impinging on activities that are necessary to maintain a robust U.S. economy that will support U.S. influence abroad.

## Debt and Private Investment

A standard proposition of elementary macroeconomics is that, in certain circumstances, government deficits can "crowd out" productive private investment. Weak private investment will, of course, slow economic growth and leave a weaker economy in the future. In standard theory, the mechanism for this is that high government borrowing leads to higher interest rates, which in turn discourage private investment. As noted in Chapter Two, however, interest rates—both nominal and real—have been falling throughout the last decade, when deficits and debt have been rising. Is government borrowing crowding out private investment?

Figure 5.1 shows the paths of gross private domestic investment and the federal government fiscal balance since the end of World War II. What is striking in the figure is the strong correlation between the two series from 1992 on. As the federal budget plunged into deficit after 2000, gross private domestic investment declined.

On the face of it, this might appear to be a case of government borrowing crowding out private investment. But here we must be particularly careful about causality. Besides laying the foundation for stronger GDP in the future, strong investment adds to current demand, increasing current output. The increased demand associated with higher investment also produces higher incomes, which, through the usual multiplier effects, bring higher demand and further increase current output. Higher current output brings higher tax revenues and, everything else being equal, a strengthened fiscal position. If investors become cautious about the future and curtail investment, the process works in reverse. So there is a mechanism for correlating levels of investment with the fiscal balance, quite independent of any effect that government borrowing may have on investment.

Alternatively, a negative shock to the economy—the financial crisis that began in late 2007 is a case in point—will depress investment as fears about the future grow. But this negative shock may also prompt stimulative fiscal measures—as happened in the United States in 2009—that weaken the government's fiscal position. Again, one will see a correlation between private investment and the government fiscal balance that does not depend on government borrowing suppressing private investment. The apparent correlation between federal deficits and private investment is evident in Figure 5.1 well before the most recent recession and the

**Figure 5.1**
**U.S. Private Investment and the Federal Fiscal Balance (Fiscal Years)**

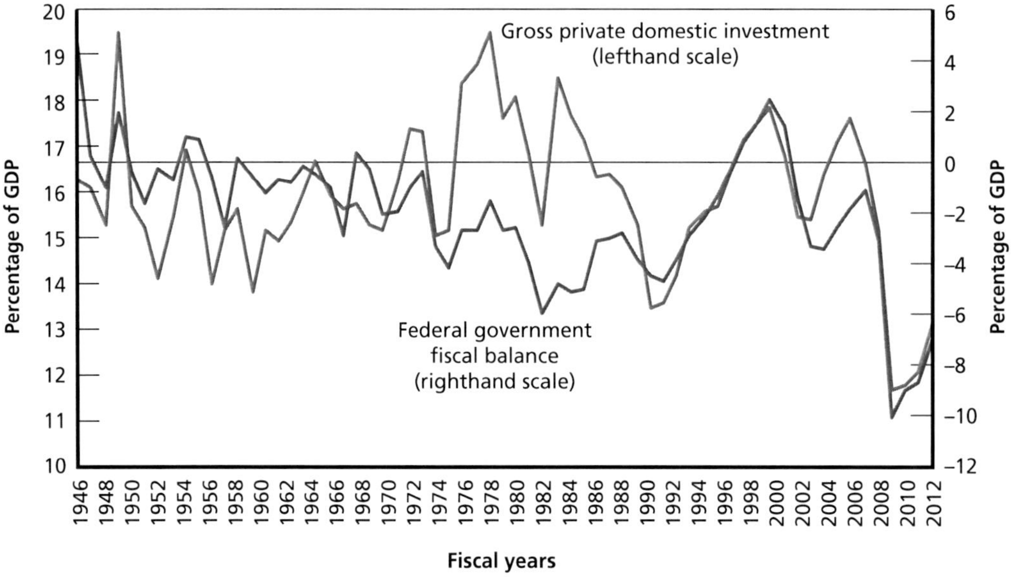


SOURCE: OMB, 2013b, Table 1.3.
RAND *RR353-5.1*

expansion of federal deficits after 2000, but this does not establish a causal link—in either direction.

We can gain another perspective by plotting the *flow* of private investment in each year against the *level* of gross general government debt (see Figure 5.2). In this figure, a negative correlation between private investment and government debt *levels* is apparent from the late 1950s onward, over multiple business cycles. The strong recovery of private investment from 2010 through 2012, while government debt was still rising as a share of GDP, breaks the pattern, however.

Clearly, government deficits and debt, private investment, and GDP growth (perhaps with a lag) are tied together in a chain of mutual causality. Reinhart, Reinhart, and Rogoff have pointed out, however, that the duration of high government debt "overhangs" can be quite long.[1] In their sample of 26 episodes of high government debt (above 90 percent of GDP) that persisted for more than five years, the authors observed that the average duration is 23 years. This long duration, they argued, "belies the view that the correlation [between high government debt and slow economic growth] is caused mainly by buildups [of debt] during business cycle recessions."[2] Further, they observe, "the long duration implies that the cumulative shortfall in output from debt overhang is potentially massive." Finally, the authors observed that growth can slow even when real interest rates do not rise. Indeed, in 11 of their 26 episodes, interest rates were not materially higher than in the period before the emergence of high government debt, but the pattern of slower growth persisted.

Just how the level of government debt constrains private investment in an environment of low real interest rates has not been satisfactorily explained, but the cases Reinhart, Reinhart,

---

1 Reinhart, Reinhart, and Rogoff, 2012.

2 Reinhart, Reinhart, and Rogoff, 2012, p. 69.

**Figure 5.2**
**U.S. Private Investment and Gross General Government Debt, by Calendar Year**

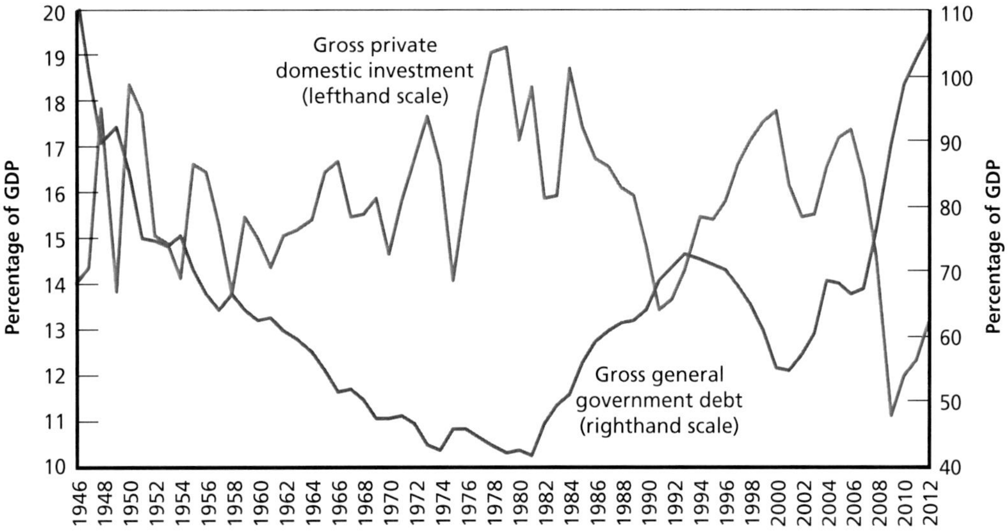


SOURCE: U.S. Department of Commerce, 2013, Table 5.1, and Federal Reserve System Board of Governors, *Release Z.1*, various dates.
RAND *RR353-5.2*

and Rogoff cited demonstrates that this can happen. An ad hoc explanation is that high levels of government debt depress investment even with low real interest rates by creating uncertainty about future taxes or changes in economic policy. Another possibility is that some sort of "financial repression"—actions of the government or monetary authorities aimed at minimizing the debt-service burden on the government—prevents interest rates from rising while simultaneously depressing private investment. The usual instruments of financial repression—what Reinhart, Reinhart, and Rogoff call "lending to the government by captive domestic audiences, explicit or implicit caps on interest rates, regulation of cross-border capital movements, and a tighter connection between government and banks through public ownership of some of the banks or through heavy 'moral suasion'"[3]—do not appear to have been present in the United States during the most recent period of increasing government debt. It is true that the U.S. government took ownership positions in some large banks during the recent financial crisis, but there is no evidence that the government used this ownership to favor bank buying of government debt at the expense of lending to private borrowers. But Reinhart and her coauthors also noted that, "In principle, 'macroprudential regulation' need not be the same as financial repression, but in practice, one can be a prelude to the other."[4] Certainly, credit standards became more stringent during and following the financial crisis.[5] This constituted

[3] Reinhart, Reinhart, and Rogoff, 2012, p. 77.

[4] Reinhart, Reinhart, and Rogoff, 2012, p. 77, fn 4.

[5] Evidence of tighter credit standards comes from the Federal Reserve's Senior Loan Officer Opinion Survey on Bank Lending Practices (Federal Reserve System Board of Governors, "Chart Data," *Senior Loan Officer Opinion Survey on Bank Lending Practices*, April 2013). The net percentage of banks reporting tighter credit standards for commercial and industrial loans (that is, the percentage of banks reporting tighter standards minus the percentage reporting loosed standards) began to rise in the late 2007, peaking at the end of 2008. The net percentage did not become negative—reflecting general loos-

a kind of financial repression in that it limited private borrowing at a time of low real interest rates. More-stringent macroprudential regulation was a consequence of the financial crisis and the regulatory problems it revealed rather than a consequence of rising government debt. Nonetheless, tighter lending standards may have offset, to some degree, the rise in interest rates that would otherwise accompany higher government borrowing. It is possible, therefore, that crowding out of private investment was happening through an alternative channel.

Whatever the causality in the relationship (if any) between government debt and private investment, Figure 5.2 is troubling. Certainly, it is difficult to tell a story that suggests that higher levels of government debt *encourage* private investment. This is a potential matter of concern, as well as a subject for future, more in-depth, exploration.

## Other Investments in the Nation's Future

Figure 5.3 illustrates the paths of federal spending for human capital development—outlays for education, training, employment services, and social services over the last 50 years and for a few years into the future.[6] These outlays are for both federally managed programs and grants to states for similar purposes. Outlays for these programs surged in FYs 2009 and 2010 as part of the fiscal stimulus measures. But the stimulus measures have now run their course, and spending fell sharply in FYs 2011 and 2012. Spending for these purposes is projected to decline further in FYs 2013 through 2018 as a consequence of the Budget Control Act and the sequester. Nonetheless, outlays for these programs will remain above their levels in the 1990s in real terms.[7]

Figure 5.4 shows federal expenditures, including grants to states for major capital projects. Spending in this budget category is dominated by military-related projects, and the fluctuations in spending for these purposes reflect different waves of military spending: the Korean War and the early Cold War in the 1950s; the Reagan defense buildup in the 1980s; and the conflicts in Iraq and Afghanistan from 2003 to 2010. Over the entire period shown in the figure, direct federal spending for capital projects not related to national defense and federal grants to states for capital projects have held roughly constant as a share of GDP. With the winding down of the conflicts in Iraq and Afghanistan, total infrastructure spending has stagnated.

---

ening of standards—until the third quarter of 2010. During the same period, virtually all reporting banks said they were charging higher spreads on commercial and industrial loans above the bank's cost of funds. Spreads also began falling in the third quarter of 2010. The survey does not ask banks by how much they tightened or eased standards or increased or decreased spreads. Thus, it is impossible to say when or if lending conditions have returned to precrisis levels. The suggestion, though, is that from late 2007 through sometime in 2011, at the earliest, credit standards were more stringent and spreads higher than before the crisis.

[6] OMB reports federal outlays for this budget category only from 1962 onwards.

[7] State governments spend more on education than does the federal government, and states are experiencing their own budget pressures. It might be reasonable, therefore, to ask what has happened to state outlays for education. Unfortunately, data to address this question are inadequate. The latest data available on state outlays for elementary and secondary education are for the 2008–2009 school year (roughly FY 2009). A short time series on state expenditures for higher education is available from State Higher Education Officers, *State Higher Education Finance Report for FY 2011*, March 14, 2012. These data show a small decline in state support for higher education, from 0.59 percent of GDP in FY 2000 to 0.51 percent in FY 2011.

**Figure 5.3**
**Federal Outlays for Human Capital Development**

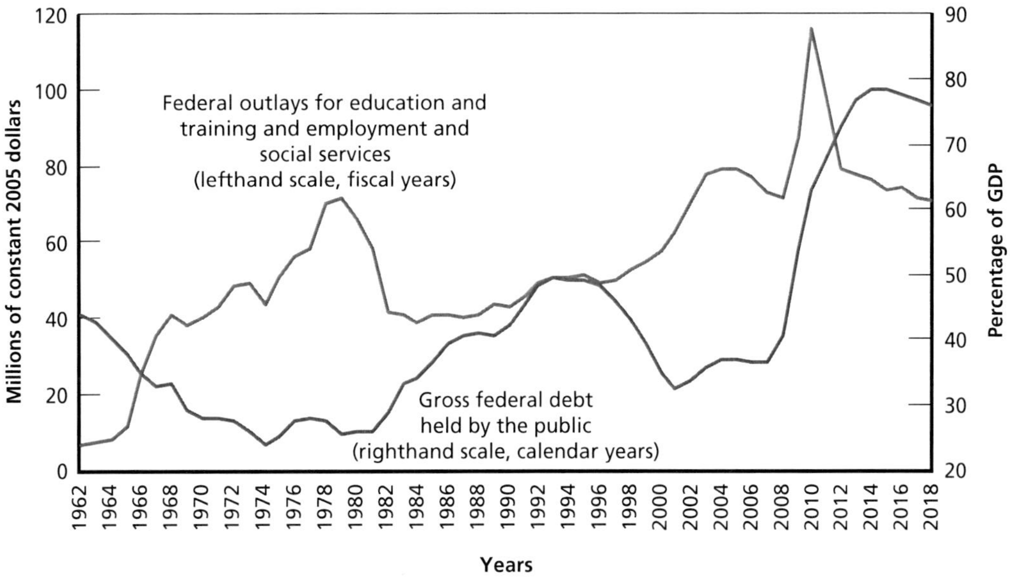


SOURCE: OMB, 2013b, Tables 7.1 and 8.8.
RAND *RR353-5.3*

**Figure 5.4**
**Federal Outlays for Major Capital Projects**

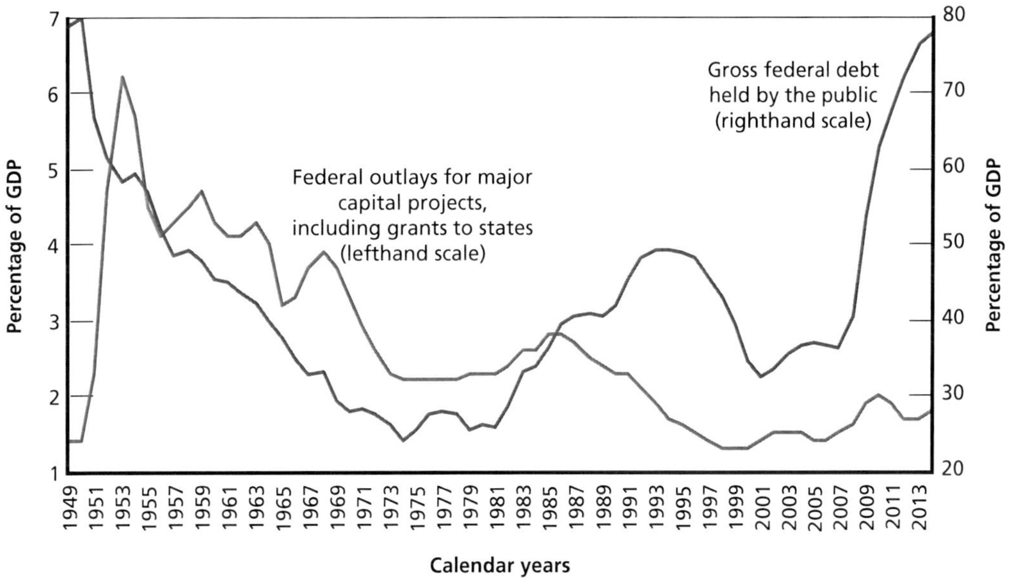


SOURCE: OMB, 2013b, Tables 7.1 and 9.3.
RAND *RR353-5.4*

Budget pressures seem not to have affected federal outlays for R&D. These outlays have fluctuated between 0.8 percent and 1.2 percent of GDP since FY 1980, without any obvious trend.[8] Unfortunately, statistics on R&D expenditures from other sources are not sufficiently current to give an indication of whether budget pressure or fiscal uncertainty has brought any retrenchment in private R&D spending. The most recent data available from the National Science Foundation provide information only through 2009.

We are left, then, with an ambiguous picture of whether high debt levels are affecting important investments in the nation's future: Gross private domestic investment shows a negative correlation with levels of government debt over much of the period since World War II, but investment has been reviving since 2009 without a reduction in government debt. Federal spending for human capital development is projected to fall in coming years but will remain above its level in the 1990s in real terms. Federal spending for major capital projects appears to have stalled, growing no faster than GDP in recent years, but this stagnation is mostly explained by the winding down of the conflicts in Iraq and Afghanistan. Federal R&D outlays continue at roughly the same level, as a share of GDP, as during the past two decades. Although there is no clear link here between high debt levels and key federal investments, neither are there any indications of rising investment.

---

8 OMB, 2013b, Table 9.7.

CHAPTER SIX

# What Might Have Happened

In the preceding chapters, we have tried to document things that have happened or that may happen in the future as a consequence of the U.S. fiscal situation or the politics surrounding it—changes in government spending patterns, economic growth rates, shares of world trade, the international role of the dollar, etc. Perhaps, however, the most important consequences of poor U.S. fiscal performance in recent years are things that *did not* happen but that might have or should have happened. Have fiscal problems caused the United States to be absent from important world affairs? Have fiscal problems undermined U.S. willingness or ability to take a lead in important international matters, deferring to other countries or simply leaving desirable actions unperformed? It is impossible to say with any certainty what might have happened if the U.S. fiscal situation had been different. Nonetheless, it may be useful to speculate about such matters.

## Exercising Economic Power

Economic power is exercised best when it is used positively to create institutions and conditions that advance U.S. national interests and simultaneously benefit the global community. Historically, the United States has used its economic strength and influence to play constructive roles in creating, shaping, or sustaining numerous important international institutions, programs, and initiatives. Major initiatives for which U.S. leadership was key include the following:[1]

- creation of the IMF, the World Bank, and the General Agreement on Tariffs and Trade
- the Bretton Woods system of exchange rates
- the Marshall Plan
- the North Atlantic Treaty Organization
- Multiple rounds of multilateral trade negotiations
- Recapitalization of the World Bank to deal with sovereign debt crises in the mid-1980s
- the Brady and the Baker Plans for the same purpose
- creation of the G-7 (later G-8)
- the Asia-Pacific Economic Cooperation Forum
- the North American Free Trade Agreement
- conversion of the General Agreement on Tariffs and Trade into the World Trade Organization (WTO)
- many international commissions, treaties, conventions, and protocols.

[1] This list is drawn, in part, from Zoellick, 2012.

In some cases, the United States used its influence to encourage or induce other nations to support these institutions, programs, or actions. Sometimes, the United States provided substantial financial support. At yet other times, the United States was sufficiently strong and self-confident to promote or preserve institutions or conditions (liberal world trade policies, for example) through its forbearance, tolerating less-than-ideal behavior from partner countries.

But what has the United States done recently? Is there any reason to link apparent failures to achieve desirable international outcomes to the U.S. government's budget situation? Predictably, the answers to these questions are mixed and ambiguous.

It is certainly possible to cite recent instances of effective use of U.S. economic power. The United States has been instrumental, for example, in organizing international sanctions against Iran. In May 2012, President Obama issued an executive order barring foreign companies and persons who assist Iran in evading multilateral sanctions from U.S. markets.[2] Rather than risk exclusion from U.S. markets, a number of prominent international firms have ceased operations in and dealings with Iran. Following the U.S. action, EU countries, led by the UK, France, and Germany, agreed in October 2012 to stringent new sanctions against Iran that added a ban on Iranian gas exports to an existing embargo of Iran oil deliveries to the EU and banned virtually all transactions between EU and Iranian banks.[3] (Germany's prominent role within the EU on this matter is particularly striking, given Germany's past reluctance to deploy its economic influence beyond Europe.) Although these sanctions have not yet dissuaded Iran from pursuing its worrying nuclear ambitions, they are imposing substantial economic costs on Iran.[4]

The United States has also made significant contributions to international financial regulation in the wake of the last financial crisis. U.S. regulators, for example, have promoted the principle of requiring systemically important financial institutions to undertake advance planning for resolving their affairs in a future crisis (so-called living wills), and the idea seems to have gained currency in Europe. On other aspects of financial regulation—separation of commercial and investment banking, proprietary trading by banks, or dealing in financial derivatives—U.S. approaches and proposals have gained less traction internationally. Attributing the apparent lack of influence on the latter matters to the U.S. fiscal position, however, would be a stretch. Certainly, the recent financial crisis has raised enough questions about the efficacy and conceptual foundations of U.S. financial regulation to explain international reluctance to follow U.S. leads in such matters.

U.S. regulators have led international efforts to enforce prohibitions against money laundering, illegal tax avoidance schemes, and violations of trade sanctions on the part of international banks and companies. Novel legal techniques, such as deferred prosecution agreements

---

[2] Executive Order 13608, Prohibiting Certain Transactions With and Suspending Entry Into the United States of Foreign Sanctions Evaders With Respect to Iran and Syria, Washington, D.C., the White House, May 1, 2012.

[3] Joshua Chaffin, "EU to Impose Tough New Sanctions on Iran," *Financial Times*, October 15, 2012.

[4] For a recent overview of international sanctions against Iran and their effects, see Kenneth Katzman, *Iran Sanctions*, Congressional Research Service, RS20871, June 2013. Iran's own economic mismanagement has no doubt contributed to its economic problems, but international sanctions have played a role in bringing about a sharp reduction in Iran's oil revenues, which in turn has undermined government finances and restricted the availability of hard currency. The Iranian currency collapsed in October 2012, and higher prices for imports and the unavailability at any price of key imported goods have pushed inflation to above 30 percent, according to official figures (Katzman, 2013, p. 55). Unofficial estimates place the inflation rate much higher. Katzman cites reports that the Iranian government has fallen behind in payments to military personnel and government workers.

and nonprosecution agreements, have emerged since 2007 as effectively streamlined measures to force international companies operating in the United States to admit failure to comply with U.S. law and to pay large settlements.[5] This approach to financial enforcement has proved sufficiently promising that the UK government has moved to enact legislation to permit similar actions there.[6]

On international macroeconomic issues, U.S. influence has been more ambiguous. The United States has not provided financial support to European institutions or to individual Eurozone nations struggling with high sovereign debt burdens. Neither, as noted in Chapter Four, has the United States pledged contingent support for the latest round of the IMF's NABs, which was motivated by the need to allow the IMF to provide interim financing to Eurozone governments. And at least in earlier stages of the Eurozone debt crisis, U.S. efforts to encourage more-coordinated action relating to the crisis were rejected in unusually blunt terms. In September 2011, for example, U.S. Treasury Secretary Timothy Geithner attended a meeting of EU finance ministers convened in Poland to discuss approaches to resolving continuing concerns over sovereign debt within the Eurozone. Geithner warned his European counterparts that the European debt crisis posed a "catastrophic risk" to international financial markets. He said that "What is very damaging is . . . the ongoing conflict between governments and the central bank," and he lectured that "[y]ou need to work together to do what is essential to the resolution of any crisis." The reaction of some European finance ministers was negative and aimed directly at U.S. fiscal problems. "I found it peculiar," the Austrian finance minister said afterward, "that even though the Americans have significantly worse fundamental data than the Eurozone, they tell us what we should do." The Swedish finance minister noted, "[w]e need to make progress, but it's quite clear the U.S. has a big problem, and the situation would be better if the U.S. could show a sustainable way forward."[7]

More recently, however, U.S. arguments in favor of strengthening demand within the Eurozone, rather than strict adherence to near-term budget-cutting measures, appear to be winning some support. On his first official visit to Europe, the new U.S. Treasury Secretary, Jacob Lew, urged his European counterparts to decide "how to better support demand," "how to better balance the pace of fiscal consolidation with the need for growth," and "how to ensure that surplus countries contribute more to demand as deficit countries undergo adjustment."[8] Shortly after Mr. Lew's remarks, the European Commission and senior policymakers in the German government signaled willingness to allow some indebted countries to stretch out their commitments to meet Eurozone targets for deficit reduction. Although final approval is still pending, technical experts within the European Commission have expressed support for Spanish proposals to move more gradually than originally planned toward budget consolidation.[9] Similarly, German Finance Minister Wolfgang Schauble indicated flexibility with regard to French plans to delay somewhat achieving the Eurozone target of a deficit of 3 percent of

---

[5] For a description of these techniques and discussion of their increasing use, see Gibson Dunn, *2012 Yearend Update on Corporate Deferred Prosecution Agreements (DPAs) and Non-Prosecution Agreements (NPAs)*, January 3, 2012.

[6] Gibson Dunn, 2012.

[7] All quotations are from Joshua Chaffin and Alex Barker, "Geithner Warns of 'Catastrophic Risk,'" *Financial Times*, September 17, 2011.

[8] Robin Harding, "Consolidation Trumps Push for Growth," *Financial Times*, April 18, 2013.

[9] Tobias Buck, "Spain Plans to Delay Deficit Reduction," *Financial Times*, April 27, 2013.

GDP.[10] It is impossible to say whether the apparent new flexibility among European policymakers regarding budget consolidation is the result of U.S. lobbying, but the timing is consistent with a renewed public push from U.S. officials in favor of more stimulative policies.

Similarly ambiguous has been U.S. leadership with respect to the international trading regime. The most recent (and still technically current) round of WTO-sponsored multilateral trade negotiations, the Doha Round, began in November 2001, just after the September 11 terrorist attacks and just before U.S. government deficits and debts began their most recent rise. These negotiations were contentious from the beginning, largely because earlier rounds of trade liberalization had already dealt with more-tractable issues. The negotiations broke down more or less for good in July 2008 (despite fitful subsequent efforts to restart them),[11] principally as a result of sharp differences among the United States, India, and China regarding agricultural trade. The collapse of these negotiations came as the United States and much of the rest of the world were struggling with a sharp contraction of economic activity, the result of the global financial crisis that began the previous year, and few governments were in a position to make concessions that might be seen as undermining production and employment in their own countries. U.S. leadership has not been sufficient to restart the Doha Round talks, let alone to conclude them, but this is likely more the result of the Great Recession and deep divisions of interest among major trading nations, rather than a consequence of the U.S. fiscal situation.

With the path to a broad multilateral trade agreement seemingly blocked, however, the United States has pursued a series of bilateral or more-limited multilateral trade agreements including agreements with Jordan (entered into force in 2001), Singapore (2004), Chile (2004), Australia (2005), Bahrain (2006), Morocco (2006), Central American states and the Dominican Republic (which includes Costa Rica, El Salvador, Guatemala, Honduras, Nicaragua, and the Dominican Republic, entering into force variously from 2006 through 2009), Oman (2009), Peru (2009), Korea (2012), and Colombia (2012). The United States is also leading larger-scale initiatives to establish a broad Pacific free-trade area (excluding China, however) and a U.S.-EU free trade arrangement. So, although progress on the Doha Round may be suffering due to lack of U.S. leadership or U.S. reluctance to accept the unbalanced terms necessary to secure agreement with other major trading partners, the United States has not been idle with respect to forging new trade alliances during the period of rising government debt.

The United States has also been active in recent years on trade-agreement enforcement initiatives, sometimes on a purely unilateral basis but sometimes leading concerted action involving multiple countries. In 2009, for example, the United States and the EU (later joined by Mexico) brought a successful complaint to the WTO against Chinese restrictions on exports of key raw materials: bauxite, coke, fluorspar, magnesium, manganese, silicon, carbide, silicon metal, yellow phosphorus, and zinc.[12] In March 2012, the United States filed a further case with the WTO, later joined by the EU and Japan, challenging Chinese export quotas, export duties, and other export restraints pertaining to rare earths, tungsten, and molybdenum.[13]

U.S. inability to support countries swept up in the revolutions of the Arab Spring, however, constitutes a clear illustration of how U.S. fiscal and economic difficulties are hamper-

---

[10] Peter Ehrlich and Hugh Carnegy, "Germans Lend Hollande Economic Backing," *Financial Times*, April 26, 2013.

[11] Alan Beattie and Frances Williams, "Doha Trade Talks Collapse," *Financial Times*, July 29, 2013.

[12] U.S. Trade Representative, *2012 USTR Report to Congress on China's WTO Compliance*, December 2012, p. 44.

[13] U.S. Trade Representative, 2012, p. 45.

ing international action that would certainly be in the U.S. interest. Secretary of State Hillary Clinton made an explicit link between the U.S. fiscal predicament and U.S. inability to support political, social, and economic transitions after the Arab Spring. In October 2011, she remarked:

> There is a democratic awakening in places that have never dreamed of democracy. And it is unfortunate that it's happening at a historic time when our own government is facing so many serious economic challenges, because there's no way to have a Marshall Plan for the Middle East and North Africa.[14]

It is easy to cite reasons that have nothing to do with the U.S. fiscal situation for why U.S. leadership on some international issues has been less than energetic or effective. A variety of domestic concerns—some but not all relating to the recent financial crisis and the subsequent recession—have absorbed resources and political capital. Although partisan divides are most visible with respect to fiscal matters, they hardly stop there. Individual observers will have to judge for themselves whether the international accomplishments of the United State during the early years of the 21st century rise to the standard set for the effective international leadership the United States demonstrated in the second half of the 20th century.

Some prominent observers see the United States withdrawing from world leadership. This phenomenon even has a catchy name: the G-zero world, a phrase coined by Ian Bremmer and David Gordon.[15] This is a play on the G-8 or G-20, groups of countries that supposedly lead the world. The G-zero world is leaderless. Other writers on international affairs have also associated U.S. reluctance to play leading roles in crises in Libya, Syria, and Mali to the U.S. government's financial policies.[16]

Failure to come to grips with fundamental issues of government finance cannot be helping U.S. international credibility. The fact that other major economies—especially the EU and Japan—are also experiencing fiscal difficulties has so far shielded the United States from the full consequences of its unsustainable fiscal situation. In a troubled world, the United States, its economy, its currency, and its financial markets still constitute safe harbors. But it would be imprudent to base U.S. fiscal policy on the assumption or the hope that difficulties elsewhere will persist indefinitely.

Fiscal problems may be undermining U.S. willingness to incur the risks inherent in international leadership and limiting the financial resources to back up international initiatives. Further, fiscal constraints are clearly diminishing the U.S. ability to make necessary adjustments at home. A variety of important domestic concerns remain unresolved—high costs for poor health care outcomes, weak public educational systems, continuing and growing income inequality, etc. None of these problems originated with the emergence of large federal deficits and government debt, but finding the necessary resources and political capital to address them is undoubtedly harder during a period of fiscal stringency. And without progress on these issues, the United States is risking the domestic social and political cohesion necessary for dealing confidently and effectively with the rest of the world.

---

[14] Steven Lee Myers, "Foreign Aid Set to Take a Hit in U.S. Budget Crisis," *New York Times*, October 3, 2011.

[15] Ian Bremmer and David Gordon, "G-Zero," *Foreign Policy*, January 7, 2011.

[16] See, for example, Francis Fukuyama, "Life in a G-Zero World," *The American Interest* blog, January 28, 2013.

These considerations have led at least one prominent commentator to ask whether anyone listens to the United States today. In a recent article, Robert Zoellick, the former president of the World Bank, wrote:

> Because the United States has not faced up to its economic problems at home, its voice on international economics does not carry, its power has waned, and its strategic designs drift with the currents of the day's news. Without healthy economic growth, the United States will be unable to lead. Just as dangerously, it will lose its identity on the global stage if it loses its economic dynamism.[17]

The evidence that current fiscal problems are undermining U.S. ability to wield international influence is ambiguous at best. We have not found clear evidence to support Zoellick's dire assessment. But neither are we in a position to refute his contentions. Certainly, it is impossible to argue that persistently high debt and political mechanisms seemingly unable to reduce this debt strengthen U.S. international influence. There is good reason to worry that this debt may harm the U.S. economy and U.S. international influence in the future. In these circumstances, it would be foolish to dismiss Zoellick's warnings.

## What Is to Be Done?

The Unites States today faces a dilemma. A persistently high level of government debt threatens future economic growth and constrains the ability of the government to pursue national interests, both international and domestic. Yet efforts to bring down the debt will further constrain government outlays and action—possibly for many years into the future. To the extent that these reductions and outlays impinge on national security programs, foreign assistance, or international representation, U.S. international influence will be diminished. If this debt brings slower economic growth, the overall U.S. economic footprint may diminish, leaving the United States with a reduced role in a variety of international economic affairs. To the extent that debt and political gridlock delay necessary domestic initiatives, they undermine the domestic cohesiveness and tranquility necessary for effective foreign action.

Economic growth will render any burden of nominal government debt more manageable, and the slow recovery that the U.S. economy has experienced since the worst of the Great Recession goes some way toward stabilizing, if not reducing, the outstanding debt as a share of GDP. But the historical record is not encouraging in this respect. After examining the experience of 44 countries, both advanced economies and emerging markets, over a span of two centuries, Reinhart and Rogoff concluded: "Seldom do countries 'grow' their way out of debts."[18] Barring some sort of default or repudiation of debt, the other options for reducing debt as a fraction of GDP are years of painful budget restraint or inflation. A recent IMF study points out that U.S. success at reducing the government debt-to-GDP ratio after World War II is in part attributable to significant bouts of "surprise inflation"—that is, inflation that was

---

[17] Zoellick, 2012.

[18] Reinhart and Rogoff, 2010, p. 577.

not foreshadowed by a prior rise in nominal interest rates—in the late 1940s and early 1950s.[19] The U.S. economy survived these periods of inflation and subsequently prospered. But this is hardly the preferred approach to debt reduction. Necessarily, surprise inflation comes at the expense of anyone holding nominal assets—traditional savers with bank accounts. Engineering surprise inflation in this era of financial markets alert to even the mildest signs of inflation would be problematic.

So, the only options are to increase government revenues or to restrain government outlays. Increasing revenue always entails some risk to production, investment, and long-term economic growth. Undoubtedly, there is some room to increase revenue through broad tax reform and elimination of unproductive tax preferences. But no plan for budget consolidation advanced to date proposes resolution of U.S. fiscal difficulties through revenue enhancement alone. Expenditures have to be cut, or their future growth significantly constrained.

But which expenditures? As we saw in Chapter Three, the costs of the conflicts in Iraq and Afghanistan contributed to the build-up of U.S. federal debt between 2001 and 2010. But the modest "peace dividend" that comes from winding down those conflicts—1.5 percent of GDP at most, depending on which military outlays are associated with those conflicts—will have been "banked" by the end of FY 2014. Further spending reductions will have to come from the base defense budget, spending for international assistance and international representation, nondefense discretionary spending, and entitlement programs. Figure 2.4 illustrated that the room for cutting base defense spending and nondefense discretionary outlays is limited. In FY 2013, these two spending categories are equivalent to less than 7 percent of GDP, less than half the share of programmatic mandatory (entitlement) spending.

From the standpoint of preserving U.S. international influence, the preferred spending reductions would be for entitlement programs. This would leave more resources for the activities that contribute directly to U.S. international influence—defense, international representation and assistance—and that create future productive capacity—investments in infrastructure, R&D, and education. Unfortunately, current legislation is exactly the reverse of this. The Budget Control Act mandates restraint in discretionary spending only; spending for entitlements is exempt from cuts. Preserving U.S. international influence will require a different approach.

---

[19] IMF, "The Good, the Bad, and the Ugly: 100 years of Dealing with Public Debt Overhangs," *World Economic Outlook*, October 2012, Ch. 3.

# References


Aghion, Philippe, David Hemous, and Enisse Kharroubi, *Cyclical Fiscal Policy, Credit Constraints, and Industry Growth*, Basel, Switzerland: Bank for International Settlements, Working Paper 340, February 2011.

Bachman, Rudiger, Steffen Elstner, and Eric Sims, "Uncertainty and Economic Activity: Evidence from Business Survey Data," *American Economic Journal: Macroeconomics*, April 2013, pp. 217–249.

Baker, Scott R., Nicholas Bloom, and Steven J. Daly, *Measuring Economic Policy Uncertainty*, Economic Policy Uncertainty website, April 29, 2013. As of June 13, 2013:
http://www.policyuncertainty.com/media/BakerBloomDavis.pdf

Bank for International Settlements, "Locational Banking Statistics," web page, June 3, 2013. As of July 8, 2013:
http://www.bis.org/statistics/bankstats.htm

———, *Triennial Survey of Foreign Exchange and Derivatives Market Activity in 2010—Final Results,* Basel, Switzerland, December 1, 2010.

Barno, David, W., Nora Bensahel, and Travis Sharp, *Hard Choices: Responsible Defense in an Age of Austerity*, Center for a New American Security, October 2011.

Basset, Laura, "Adm. Mike Mullen: 'National Debt Is Our Biggest Security Threat,'" *Huffington Post*, June 24, 2010.

Beattie, Alan, and Frances Williams, "Doha Trade Talks Collapse," *Financial Times*, July 29, 2013.

BIS—*See* Bank for International Settlements.

"Bob Carr Denies Romney Diplomatic Gaffe," *Australian Times*, July 23, 2012. As of July 8, 2012:
http://www.australiantimes.co.uk/news/australia-world-news/bob-carr-denies-romney-diplomatic-gaffe.htm

Bremmer, Ian, and David Gordon, "G-Zero," *Foreign Policy*, January 7, 2011. As of June 13, 2013:
http://eurasia.foreignpolicy.com/posts/2011/01/07/g_zero

Buck, Tobias, "Spain Plans to Delay Deficit Reduction," *Financial Times*, April 27, 2013.

Bureau of Labor Statistics, "CPI for All Urban Consumers," database, undated. As of July 8, 2013:
http://data.bls.gov/cgi-bin/surveymost?bls

Cassata, Donna, "Panetta Warns of 'Disaster' from Defense Cuts," *Associated Press*, June 13, 2012.

CBO—*See* Congressional Budget Office.

Cecchetti, Stephen G., M. S. Mohanty, and Fabrizio Zampolli, *The Real Effects of Debt*, Basel, Switzerland: Bank for International Settlements, Working Paper 352, September 2011.

Chaffin, Joshua, "EU to Impose Tough New Sanctions on Iran," *Financial Times*, October 15, 2012.

Chaffin, Joshua, and Alex Barker, "Geithner Warns of 'Catastrophic Risk.'" *Financial Times*, September 17, 2011.

Congressional Budget Office, *The Budget and Economic Outlook Fiscal Years 2013 to 2023*, Washington, D.C., February 5, 2013.

Congressional Budget Office, *Updated Budget Projections: Fiscal Years 2013 to 2023*, Washington, D.C., May 14, 2013. As of June 17, 2013:
http://www.cbo.gov/publication/44172

Defense Advisory Committee, *A New U.S. Defense Strategy for a New Era: Military Superiority, Agility, and Efficiency*, Stimson, November 2012.

DoD—*See* U.S. Department of Defense.

Economic Policy Uncertainty, U.S. Monthly Index, database, various dates. As of July 9, 2013:
http://www.policyuncertainty.com/us_monthly.html

Ehrlich, Peter, and Hugh Carnegy, "Germans Lend Hollande Economic Backing," *Financial Times*, April 26, 2013.

Eurostat, Interest Rates, "EMU Convergence Criterion Series—Monthly Data," data table, June 12, 2013.

Executive Order 13608, Prohibiting Certain Transactions With and Suspending Entry Into the United States of Foreign Sanctions Evaders With Respect to Iran and Syria, Washington, D.C., the White House, May 1, 2012.

Federal Reserve System Board of Governors, "Price-Adjusted Broad Dollar Index—Monthly Index," in *Foreign Exchange Rates—H.10*, historical data, July 1, 2013. As of July 25, 2013:
http://www.federalreserve.gov/releases/h10/summary/indexbc_m.htm

———, "Flow of Funds Accounts of the United States: Historical Data," in *Release Z.1, Financial Accounts of the United States*, various dates. As of July 9, 2013:
http://www.federalreserve.gov/releases/z1/Current/data.htm

———, *Release H.15, Selected Interest Rates: Historical Data*, various dates. As of July 9, 2013:
http://www.federalreserve.gov/releases/h15/data.htm

———, "Chart Data," *Senior Loan Officer Opinion Survey on Bank Lending Practices*, April 2013. As of July 9, 2013:
http://www.federalreserve.gov/boarddocs/SnLoanSurvey/201305/chartdata.htm

Fukuyama, Francis, "Life in a G-Zero World," *The American Interest* blog, January 28, 2013. As of June 1, 2013:
http://blogs.the-american-interest.com/fukuyama/2013/01/28/life-in-a-g-zero-world/

Gibson Dunn, *2012 Yearend Update on Corporate Deferred Prosecution Agreements (DPAs) and Non-Prosecution Agreements (NPAs)*, January 3, 2012.

Giles, Chris, "Austerity Is Hurting, But Is It Working?" *Financial Times*, April 27, 2013.

Harding, Robin "Consolidation Trumps Push for Growth," *Financial Times*, April 18, 2013.

Heniff, Bill, Jr., Elizabeth Rybicki, and Shannon M. Mahan, *The Budget Control Act of 2011*, Washington, D.C.: Congressional Research Service, R41965, August 2011.

Herndon, Thomas, Michael Ash, and Robert Pollin, *Does High Public Debt Consistently Stifle Economic Growth? A Critique of Reinhart and Rogoff*, Political Economy Research Institute, University of Massachusetts Amherst, Working Paper Number 322, April 2013.

International Bank for Reconstruction and Development, World Development Indicators, database, April 16, 2013. As of July 9, 2013:
http://data.worldbank.org/data-catalog/world-development-indicators

International Monetary Fund, Currency Composition of Official Foreign Exchange Reserves (COFER), database, Washington, D.C., March 29, 2013. As of July 9, 2013:
http://www.imf.org/external/np/sta/cofer/eng/

———, *Fiscal Monitor: Fiscal Adjustment in an Uncertain World*, Washington, D.C., April 2013.

———, "IMF Managing Director Christine Lagarde Welcomes Additional Pledges to Increase IMF Resources, Bringing Total Commitments to US$456 Billion," Washington, D.C., press release, No. 12/231, June 19, 2012. As of June 17, 2013:
http://www.imf.org/external/np/sec/pr/2012/pr12231.htm

———, "IMF Managing Director Christine Lagarde Welcomes Pledges from Algeria and Brunei Darussalam to Boost Fund Resources," press release, Washington, D.C., No. 12/388, October 13, 2012. As of June 17, 2013: http://www.imf.org/external/np/sec/pr/2012/pr12388.htm

———, "The Good, the Bad, and the Ugly: 100 years of Dealing with Public Debt Overhangs," *World Economic Outlook,* October 2012.

IMF—*See* International Monetary Fund.

Katzman, Kenneth, *Iran Sanctions*, Congressional Research Service, RS20871, June 2013. As of August 13, 2013:
http://www.fas.org/sgp/crs/mideast/RS20871.pdf

Kumar, Mohan, and Jaejoon Woo, *Public Debt and Growth*, working paper, International Monetary Fund, WP/10/174, July 1, 2010.

Mandel, Benjamin R., "Why Is the U.S. Share of World Merchandise Exports Shrinking?" *Current Issues in Economics and Finance*, Vol. 18, No. 1, 2012.

Myers, Steven Lee, "Foreign Aid Set to Take a Hit in U.S. Budget Crisis," *New York Times*, October 3, 2011.

Office of Management and Budget, *Budget of the United States, Fiscal Year 2014*, April 2013a.

———, *The President's Budget for Fiscal Year 2014, Historical Tables*, April 2013b.

O'Hanlon, Michael, *A Moderate Plan for Additional Defense Budget Cuts*, Washington, D.C.: The Brookings Institution, February 2013.

OMB—*See* Office of Management and Budget.

Posen, Adam, "Japan Should Rethink Its Stimulus," *Financial Times*, January 16, 2013.

Public Law 107-16, Economic Growth and Tax Relief Reconciliation Act of 2001.

Public Law 108-27, Jobs and Growth Tax Relief Reconciliation Act of 2003.

Public Law 112-25, Budget Control Act of 2011.

Public Law 113-6, Consolidated and Further Continuing Appropriations Act, 2013.

Reinhart, Carmen M., Vincent R. Reinhart, and Kenneth S. Rogoff, "Public Debt Overhangs: Advanced Economy Episodes Since 1800," *Journal of Economic Perspectives*, Summer 2012, pp. 69–86.

Reinhart, Carmen M., and Kenneth S. Rogoff, "Growth in a Time of Debt," *American Economic Review: Papers and Proceedings*, Vol. 100, No. 2, May 2010, pp. 573–578.

———, *This Time Is Different: Eight Centuries of Financial Folly*, Princeton University Press, 2009.

State Higher Education Officers, *State Higher Education Finance Report for FY 2011*, March 14, 2012. As of June 13, 2013:
http://www.sheeo.org/resources/publications/shef-%E2%80%94-state-higher-education-finance-fy11

Subramanian, Arvind, and Martin Kessler, *The Renminbi Bloc Is Here: Asia Down, Rest of the World to Go?* Washington, D.C.: Peterson Institute of International Economics, Working Paper 12-19, October 2012.

U.S. Department of Commerce, Bureau of Economic Analysis, *National Income and Product Accounts Tables*, webpage, May 2013. As of July 9, 2013:
http://www.bea.gov/iTable/iTable.cfm?ReqID=9&step=1#reqid=9&step=1&isuri=1

———, *International Transactions*. webpage, May 2013. As of July 9, 2013:
http://www.bea.gov/iTable/iTable.cfm?ReqID=6&step=1#reqid=6&step=1&isuri=1

U.S. Department of Defense, *Sustaining U.S. Global leadership: Priorities for 21st Century Defense*, Washington, D.C., January 2012.

———, *FY 2014 Green Book*, Washington, D.C., May 2013.

U.S. Department of Defense, Office of the Under Secretary of Defense (Comptroller), *Fiscal Year 2013 Budget Request*, February 2012.

———, *Fiscal Year 2014 Budget Request and FY 2013 Update*, Washington, D.C., April 2013a.

———, *News Briefing by Under Secretary of Defense Hale and Lt. General Ramsay on the Fiscal Year Defense Budget Proposal*, Washington, D.C., April 10, 2013b.

U.S. Department of Defense, Statistical Information Analysis Division, *DoD Personnel and Procurement Statistics*, website, various dates. As of July 9, 2013:
http://siadapp.dmdc.osd.mil/

U.S. Department of State, *Department of State Operations Congressional Budget Justification*, Washington, D.C., various dates. As of July 9, 2013:
http://www.state.gov/s/d/rm/rls/statecbj/index.htm

U.S. Department of the Treasury, "Major Foreign Holders of Treasury Securities," April 30, 2013. As of July 9, 2013:
www.treasury.gov/resource-center/data-chart-center/tic/documents/mfhhis01.txt

———, *Monthly Statement of the Public Debt (MSPD) and Downloadable Files*, database, July 5, 2013. As of July 9, 2013:
http://www.treasurydirect.gov/govt/reports/pd/mspd/mspd.htm

U.S. Trade Representative, *2012 USTR Report to Congress on China's WTO Compliance*, December 2012, p. 44.

Zoellick, Robert, "The Currency of Power," *Foreign Policy*, November 2012, pp. 67–73.